TOMÁS TAVEIRA

Architectural Monographs No 37

TOMÁS TAVEIRA

A.D. ACADEMY EDITIONS

Acknowledgements

I would like to thank my daughter Silvia and my son Ricardo for their support. I am also grateful to my friends António Pedro, Jorge Rangel, António Consiglieri Pedroso, António Portela, Alderico Santos Machado, Fernando Martins, Raul Martins, António Machado Rodrigues and José Troufa Real.

Cover: Portuguese Parliament Building, Lisbon

Art Editor: Andrea Bettella
House Editor: Maggie Toy
Editorial Team: Iona Spens, Pip Vice

First published in Great Britain in 1994 by
ACADEMY EDITIONS
An imprint of the Academy Group Ltd
Editorial Offices
42 Leinster Gardens London W2 3AN
Member of VCH Publishing Group

ISBN 1 85490 335 7 (HB)
ISBN 1 85490 336 5 (PB)

Distributed in the United States of America in 1994 by
ST MARTIN'S PRESS
175 Fifth Avenue, New York, NY 10012

Printed and bound in Singapore

CONTENTS

Whatever else you think of Tomás Taveira you can see from the pictures that he is an exuberant designer. Forms and colours come tumbling out from some great cornucopia of ideas for buildings, furniture, ornaments, sets for television and so on. There is a vivid imagination at work, a keen intelligence, an irrepressible sense of fun, a celebration of sheer joy in the act of designing. The public of Lisbon adores his work; it flocks to his buildings in large numbers. Some architects and critics find them vulgar and overwrought. Why? And why does Taveira permit himself to alienate them?

He can't help it. Exuberance is there and it cannot be subdued. Then there's Taveira's development which I traced in an earlier book; I have to tread carefully here to risk irritating those who have read it whilst giving detail for those who have not. [1] Taveira is a self-made designer from what he calls a 'blue collar' background. He joined an architect's office in 1955, as a general dogsbody, and proved to have a 'golden hand' for drawing; which he certainly retains. Three years on from high-school education, he joined Architecture at the Lisbon School of Fine Arts. To a certain extent he was a dissident, and since Portugal in the 1950s still had its Fascist dictator, Salazar, Taveira, was drafted after a year into the army, which proved very formative. As an avid reader he met Portugal's leading poet, Herberto Helder, a librarian like Philip Larkin. Helder's musings on architecture have stayed with Taveira. 'Architecture,' said Helder, 'is not a natural thing. It comes from thinking; from elaboration by the brain. So it has to be adapted to history, and to the locality (of its building).' A pioneering statement of Contextualism!

An almost fatal accident left Taveira immobilised and, during months of convalescence, all he could do was go to the cinema. There he saw Joseph Losey's *Eva* some 75 times and the Rome of Losey, of Bernini and Michelangelo reinforced Helder's views on history and locality. Moreover, Losey's use of light to generate atmosphere raised seeds in Taveira's mind: 'if our emotions can be so affected by light in film, then why not in architecture?' Visconti's *Senso* – which Taveira saw some 40 times – taught him the *control* of light; and he learned the *structuring* of space from Wim Wenders' *Paris-Texas*.

Thus cinema proved formative for Taveira; so did the open spaces of Whitman's poetry and Allen Ginsberg's *Howl*; the sheer sense of liberation as John dos Passos moved, free-wheeling, across America; liberation too in Jack Kerouac's *On the Road*. It seemed to Taveira that in comparison to all of

these there was something cramped and crushing about the 'spaces' of the Modern Movement.

This of course came in many kinds, from the 'spaces between the floor and multi-level ceilings' of early Wright to the blank open 'sheds' with curtain wall of the later Mies. Le Corbusier had described the 'orthodox version' in his seminal Five Points (*Les Cinq Points d'une Architecture Nouvelle*) in which 'space' was clamped between horizontal slabs supported by columns with minimal, probably glass, external walls. Pevsner had sold that 'entire facade conceived in glass' to the public in his *Pioneers of the Modern Movement* of 1936, where he described the Fagus Offices by Gropius as simple, rectangular and flat roofed, the glassy facades supported only by 'narrow bands of steel' which opened up the interiors to the 'great universe of space outside'; but also let in excessive solar heat. Nor could there be a sense, given these 'leaky' facades, of internal space modelled as three-dimensional walk-in 'sculpture!' As for Le Corbusier's version; his construction made it difficult to penetrate the concrete slabs and thus model space up into the third dimension. All we got was SLEBS: Spaces Left Empty Between the Slabs; divided into rooms by partitions; simple, rectangular and dull with no way of controlling the light to 'model' space in the ways that Taveira had learned from the various films.

But Pevsner also had a moral programme. He insisted that the Fagus Offices set the 'one true style' for the 20th century. Simple, rectangular, anonymous building of the kind that could be designed for factory production and conceived, not for the whims of eccentric clients but for 'the people' in the mass. Social responsibility demanded that buildings should be cold, hard and anonymous; anything else was self-indulgence, the architect's expression as a prima donna. Even in the 20s there had been Expressionism, with its strange curves and jagged angles. But those days were over, part of history and for two generations architecture became simple, rectangular and dull. Few architects would dare to be branded 'antisocial?'

There was a strange alliance between methods of construction; using rectangular frames and abstract art of a kind – represented by Mondrian – which I call 'geometric construction'. But Pevsner's Fagus, all along, had been a rather sterile fiction. There *were* no narrow bands of steel; the supporting structure indeed was hefty brick piers with entasis-like Doric columns. There were those problems of solar over-heating. Pevsner had described an *ideology*; this is how buildings ought to be; nothing at all to do with built reality!

Yet, ever since, there has been a Puritan lobby claiming the high moral ground for simple, geometric abstraction in architecture. 'Simple forms for simple minds' as Taveira puts it, using the latter-day term of Minimalism. But what is there so profound, so intellectually honest about cramming functions that may not fit into simple, rectangular boxes? Surely more creative challenge, intellectual challenge, too, exists in fitting forms around functions, designing for sensory delight. Most experience of building is through the senses; how perverse to design in such a sterile way that denies those senses!

Given that these are basic human needs it is hardly surprising that by 1960 there were reactions against such abstraction. Pevsner in a postscript to his *Pioneers* was indeed furious with those who had let down the Puritan, abstract geometry side; such as the Le Corbusier of Ronchamp, the Brazilians with their structural acrobatics; this craving of architects for individual expression of the public, for the surprising and the fantastic, for an escape out of reality into a fairy world. As mentioned already Pevsner's idea of Fagus was a fairy world. And he never did explain why, if the public really craved for the surprising and the fantastic, critics such as he should want to deny them. If you claim the moral high ground of *serving* society then surely you take heed of what society wants? There is no way in which you *serve* society by imposing an arrogant: 'We know what is best for you!'

In his final broadside on such matters, a radio broadcast of 1966, Pevsner tellingly compared Stirling and Gowan's Leicester Engineering Building with Gollins, Melvin and Ward's Arts Tower in Sheffield. Certain forms at Leicester follow their functions rather well; the sloping underside to the lecture theatre, circulation that tapers within the height of the tower where fewer and fewer people go. Yet for Pevsner the jagged angles made Leicester Expressionist; he much preferred the functional sub-Miesian Sheffield Tower in which I was working at the time; and thus knew its horrendous problems of a *functional* kind; desperate solar overheating, heat loss, wind blown to a dreadful vortex at the entrance and circulation that had tapered off just at the point where it was needed most for the two roof-top lecture theatres.

This is when I realised that in Pevsner-speak, 'functional', described merely the *appearance* of buildings; the simple, cool rectilinear qualities of his 'one true' abstract style which had nothing at all to do with how the building actually worked.

Expressionist by contract meant wilful and sculptural, whereas even in the 20s there had been far more to it than that. Indeed, Finsterlin designed amazing sculpture; but there were others whose non-rectangular forms really did develop out of functional considerations, such as Häring's farm at Gut Garkaü!

TAVEIRA'S EARLY WORK

Like the rest of us Taveira is a child of his time and much of his early work consists of social housing; concrete-prefabricated for anonymous clients. Pevsner would have been proud of him. That was true of enormous estates around Lisbon, such as Alfragide (1969); Troia and Sesimbra (1970); Olaias, started in 1972, Chelas (1975); João XXI (1978) and Benfica (1979). Yet, increasingly, the housing became more generous, more personal, more colourful, more modelled in three dimensions, more actively 'Expressionist'. Taveira had been set thinking, as had every other architect with a lively mind, by the three great books of 1966: Aldo Rossi's *Architecture of the City*, Robert Venturi's *Complexity and Contradiction in Architecture*, Reyner Banham's 'bumper' volume *The New Brutalism*. It was Banham, indeed, who affected Taveira most; especially in his treatment of James Stirling. It was even Stirling's prefabricated work, evident in his Runcorn Housing for example – with its washing machine windows – that stimulated Taveira into doing such things as the João XXI housing.

Most of all though, it was the Leicester Building which had proved so difficult for Pevsner. Much of it derives from the red-brick vernacular of Lancashire mills with their glass towers, or rope-races, containing drive belts to the various floors from their basement steam engines. Here, indeed, there was a Helder-like drawing on the past; but what really struck Taveira was Stirling and Gowan's escape stair: a spiral within a glazed octagon which, delicate as it was, could by no means support the weight of the theatre above. From this Taveira derived a maxim: form indeed may follow function as it does there; but it may also 'follow fun'.

So it was that Taveira once and for all rejected the puritanism of Pevsner; the Gropius of Fagus and Le Corbusier's SLEBS. There is vigorous modelling of three-dimensional space in his Balaia Hotel and bungalows at Albufeira (1968-70) with, in the spirit of the films that had moved him, particular attention to the light of the Algarve. What's more, such things as entrances are marked by a Venturi-like exuberance of Pop signs and Las Vegas-like neon; the kind of Pop Taveira also displayed in his Record Shop at Cascais (1969-70). The plan is a reduction of Michelangelo's St Peter's with semi-circular corners providing bays for different kinds of music and equipment. There are super-graphic rainbow murals by Sa Nogueira incorporating Herberto Helder's poetry.

Taveira's projects became larger and bolder, often still in a somewhat Brutalist vein as in the Castil Building – offices and shopping – in Lisbon (1967-72); the Valentim de Carvalho Record Plant (1968-70); the Don Carlos Building of 1973-83. This was his first gesture towards High-Tech with diagonal external bracing. There had been a Revolution – anti Salazar – and as in most states after such a trauma, Portugal's economy slumped low. So there was no steel for Taveira's 'outriggers'; he had to make them of concrete which wasn't at all the point. Yet still, as one approaches Lisbon from Belèm, Don Carlos looks 'right' next to the dockside cranes. I argued in the previous book also that some of the detail: a rooftop aedicule, a 'frozen' cascade of water – a painted version, as it were, of Ledoux from Arc-et-Senans – Taveira's *Art Deco* lights further homage to Stirling's Leicester staircase – and so on – may have been the first pieces *ever* of Post-Modern!

Since Olaias was started in 1973, however, it has acted as Taveira's test bed and indeed continues to do so. Taveira has moved into one of his own apartments – he likes the spaces he designed – but few architects surely *dare* live so directly on the job. Olaias is rather more than housing. There is a shopping mall, an hotel, offices, a sports and leisure club; everything one needs for day-to-day living; including, it has to be said, architecture. Prefabricated, as much of it may be, this is no Pevsnerian exercise in flatness, greyness and dullness. Bold modelling and colour put paid to that; indeed the various blocks end in super-graphic rainbows. The Shopping Mall of course is modelled up and into the third dimension with Taveiran roof-lanterns for the control of light, whilst the entrance to the Mall is by a semi-circular colonnade, with pediments, and again Las Vegas neon.

Olaias has been transformed over the years, with increasing elaborations, and so was Taveira's Satellite Building started in 1972. Taveira thought in terms of glassy-blackness and it could have been a simple Miesian tower, straight up and down with I-sections of the kind that Mies clipped onto the Seagram Building. The Satellite has steppings of a Sears' Tower kind, and in the ten year period of gestation Taveira enhanced that articulation, not to mention a sense of scale, with red support-

ing columns near the ground; no useless I's of a Seagram kind, and pediments, too, to terminate the Sears-like shafts.

In ten years, therefore, Taveira changed from Modern to Post-Modern and in the same ten years he was creating, opposite the Satellite Building, his largest and most complete architectural 'statement' to date: Amoreiras. Amoreiras is a Lisbon landmark indeed; a counterweight across the City to the old Castle of S Jorge and unmistakable as you fly on a good day into the airport of Portelo de Sacavém.

It has a huge, triangular plinth; its hypotenuse some 320 metres long. Alongside are three 16-storey towers in black glass. The outer ones have huge, squared-off Doric capitals, surmounted by pink parapets pierced on each side by absent pediments. The central tower has no such capital; it has truncated black glass cones, inverted and Egyptian in character. The towers have been compared to huge chess pieces: a Queen, as it were, between two Kings.

The triangle's right-angled corner lies some 216 metres to the south, and 10 storeys of housing loom over it in an L-shaped formation; curtain walled in both medieval and modern senses. Its curtains are pierced by circular glass towers – derived yet again from the Leicester staircase – disposed rhythmically along its sides and punctuated at the corners by rather larger towers with slotted, cylindrical capitals. Some see affinities with the Bofill of Marne la Vallée and elsewhere, but Taveira's towers are less repetitive and indeed more site-specific. His corner-clusters derive – including their colours – from column-clusters in the great baroque churches of Lisbon, especially San Antonio.

Once we come down to earth, Amoreiras takes on a different aspect. Its street facades are articulated by colonnades, panels with circular Stirling windows; entries and other features marked by arches, geometricised pediments and other features in warm browns, pinks, ochres, yellows and whites derived yet again from Lisbon's very special baroque. Amoreiras contains some 350 shops, 12 cinemas, and even a chapel with 1,200 parking spaces underground. This by no means accounts for the busy throng of people that always seems to enliven Amoreiras. They come flooding in, certainly by car; but also by bus and taxi. Amoreiras is *the* place to be in Lisbon, to the detriment it seems of traditional shopping centres. After its completion in 1986, Lisbon took Amoreiras to its heart; very quickly it became an urban marker; a monument in Aldo Rossi's sense. It was soon featured in the local guide books – the *only* building included that was post-baroque. Now its in the international guides; meriting a star indeed for Baedeker. Without resorting to Heidegger, or even to Norberg-Schulz, with their earth and sky, their mortals and their divinities he has obviously created a sense of *place* to which ordinary people respond!

Perhaps the culmination of this phase is Taveira's Banco Ultramarino (1983-89). Taveira worked within an envelope, designed already for housing. His first sketches show Amoreiras-like detail, but he probed further into the heritage of Lisbon; the horseshoe arches of the nearby bullring, the flared forms of the guitars on which the Fado is played: inspiration indeed for Taveira's pink and blue towers, wide and narrow, with their flaring tops containing keystones.

These rise from a complex Taveira plinth with blue glass slabs between them. Taveira's plinth contains his splendid banking hall with its wave-form counter; invention of a kind which permeates the building as a whole. For, given the budget of a bank, Taveira's details are quite exquisite! Form follows function, indeed, but Taveira's alternation of solid towers and blue glass walls means that few recent banks have fitted their functions quite so well in terms of offering varied kinds of accommodation; rooms for private conversations with clients, rooms for small teams working together, with lighting levels according to their kind of work; particularly right for computer screens and so on!

So increasingly Taveira heeded Helder, adapting his buildings 'to history, and to the locality'. Thus they became Contextual; by no means in the sense of matching what was there, but in terms of forms, colours and other features deriving directly from the context, developed in new and imaginative ways. These buildings unequivocally are of Lisbon; they would have been alien in any other place. So why are they not described as 'regional'; the proper term, surely, for buildings *of* a specific place?

CRITICAL REGIONALISM

By the time Amoreiras was completed, the word 'regional' was highjacked by Kenneth Frampton for his 'Critical Regionalism'. A new – almost Pevsner-like – 'solemnity' was setting in; architecture, again had to be abstract. Frampton had written in 1982 on: *The Isms of Contemporary Architecture*. Jencks-like, he categorised a number of these including 'Neo-Productivism' with its emphasis on factory production, machine-forms for

living in and so on. Taveira's prefabricated work, even Don Carlos, no doubt fitted within this 'ism'. Frampton's second was neo-Rationalism; the simple, white abstractions of early Rossi; source perhaps of much later Minimalism. Then there was Structuralism; a Team-X structuring of the city which had nothing at all to do with French intellectual tendencies and that 'Critical Regionalism' which Frampton claimed as adding something new. Truth to tell, Frampton was torn between conflicting beliefs; opposing ideologies indeed: his deeply held Socialist distaste for any kind of centralised power, as represented by multi-national corporations, and his equally firm commitment to that pure, simple, rectangular, *abstract* architecture that Pevsner had declared to be the one, true style. Frampton, like Pevsner, had made his reputation as historian/exponent of such abstraction.

Frampton has stated clearly his political aim; to deconstruct universal Modernism. What's more, to replace it with localised images quintessentially rooted in each region. Most of us would have thought: clearly vernacular, but that, for Frampton, was far too Populist. Perhaps he found it redolent of Disney? But at least one might have expected that quintessentially rooted might mean drawing on the local climate, the topography, on deeply-rooted cultural concerns. But not a bit of it. Such concerns would compromise what Frampton really loved; the purity of abstract, simple, minimal forms. He presented three particular heroes: the Mexican Barragán, the Swiss (Ticino) Botta and the Portuguese (from Oporto) Siza.

Barragán, in his early houses had 'made a subtle move away from the universal reductive syntax of the International Style'; does Frampton mean 'simple abstract forms'? Yet his work retained that abstract sense of objecthood which has characterised the art of our era. Well yes, there has been quite a lot of geometric abstraction!

But Barragán is a special case; for despite the objecthood of his forms, there is a sense of place in his work; dependent on his glowing colours, landscaping, those forms overgrown with exuberant vegetation. Not to say a sense, from Barragán's grouping of those forms, of a *picturesque* surprise around the corner. Yet while Frampton promoted his three stars equally, it is Botta and Siza rather than Barragán who emerge as the stars of Regionalism. Clearly Barragán is far too colourful, too concerned with human values, too expressive of his soul for those who look for intellectual rigour in Frampton's Critical Regionalism.

Yet despite such intellectual pretensions, Frampton declares

his Critical Regionalism to be ideologically ill-defined
. . . rather marginal but nonetheless distinct; for of course there is a fundamental problem. As Tom Wolfe suggests, so engagingly, the abstraction of the International Style – in architecture – was first exposed at the Bauhaus and then, on a very much larger scale, in German social housing of the 20s; some of it indeed by Gropius: *From Bauhaus to Our House* as Wolfe, so accurately, puts it. But as Gropius, Mies and others ejected by the Nazis started after the war to rebuild America in their image they translated the abstraction of the Bauhaus into the one and only style for those very multi-national corporations which Frampton despises so much. Their building of filing cabinets for humans surely is the ultimate expression of Frampton's 'abstract . . . objecthood'.

At the time of writing, in 1982, Frampton's Critical Regionalists had never built on such a scale. Little more than modest houses, small apartment blocks and so on had been executed. Critical Regionalism was, rather, a somewhat muddled attempt to promote simple, abstract, Minimalism architecture as somehow *intellectually* profound; which exasperates Taveira to distraction: the rejection of everything to do with context, this reduction of architecture to the simplest and dullest of forms, the most subdued of colours and so on. Botta's House at Ligornetto is such a piece of 'abstract . . . objecthood'; simple, indeed naive in its geometry which places the major openings facing a cabbage patch and leaves the tiniest of slit windows facing the major open view! How can that be seen as 'intellectual'? If such emperors have any clothes at all then that clothing is as Minimal as their buildings!

THE FUNDAMENTALISTS

Yet Pluralist as he is – like all Post-Modernists – Taveira respects Frampton's intentions; finds indeed that the latter loves – in private – architecture of complexity and colour; architecture even as an expression of soul. Barragán, after all, was one of his stars. But on a public platform things are different; Frampton resumes his politicised, aggressively Minimalist stance – forced to do so, in Taveira's view by simple-minded disciples who simply want to *know* the truth. When you think about it there has been a consistent strain. The abstractionists, the Minimalists, those who have sought a very pure, simple architecture, disparaging entirely the fitting of form to function, have never brooked any opposition: Gropius, Pevsner, Mies, the neo-Rationalists, the Critical Regionalists; they always *knew*

the one true style and everyone else was therefore wrong.

But why such narrow-minded views? According to Taveira, abstraction, in the form of Minimalism, has no *intellectual* substance whatsoever: anyone can draw its simple geometries, there is no mental effort expended! Moreover, it ignores the pragmatics of space, to do with temperatures, acoustics, lighting and so on. Nor has it anything to do with the users' basic comfort, let alone sophisticated pleasures. It is an architecture of nothing, so it has to resort to codified rules and sanctions; it has had to become a matter of faith rather than reason: we know the truth and everyone else is wrong!

Which of course happens with religions, wherein the fundamentalists so hate those of other faiths that they kill them. And in architecture too; though rarely do our fundamentalists actually murder, they aim to kill careers instead. In the days of Ernesto Rogers, *Casabella* was a Pluralist journal as indeed *AS* is to this day. But that is becoming fairly rare indeed. When Gregotti succeeded Ernesto Rogers the shutters came down. *Casabella* became a vehicle of propaganda for neo-Rationalism and the other abstract Minimalisms that followed.

Taveira perceives the editors of journals to be fundamentalists, competition juries loaded with the faithful and so on. They promote this very narrow, abstract Minimalist work and censor out anything more complex. I suggested to Taveira that he see them as 'ayatollahs', issuing their murderous 'fatwas'; to which his reply was: 'absolutely!'

In religion at least the 'ayatollahs' have had some kind of education; their architectural equivalent have not. Few are architects at all; nor art critics, historians, scholars, even philosophers. They are just journalists who find architecture a fairly easy write. Lacking as they do any kind of culture, they can only work to formulae. So, simple-minded as they are, they look for simple architecture too which these days is abstract Minimalism. But if that is all you publish then you deny your readers any chance of contrast, to decide *for themselves* what they'd rather have. If you publish elephants *and* peacocks they then decide which they prefer; possibly neither, in which case they think of other things. But if your publication is devoted entirely to elephants then that is all your readers will see; there *will* be no choices they can make.

I point out that in England we too have our 'ayatollahs'; in the popular press, on radio and on television; in our professional journals – with exceptions – in competition juries and so on. In the award givers even of RIBA Gold Medals our 'ayatollahs' have their knee-jerk reactions against anything that might be called Post-Modern. But they are not Minimalist either: they are, rather Maximalist; promoting those complexities of structure known as High-Tech! Which is no threat at all for Taveira – think of Don Carlos. But High-Tech means so little outside England that he sees it as a refreshing change; a well-wrought extension to architectural *expression* but nothing at all to do with extending our *technical* skills!

So in Britain, as in southern Europe, architecture has its 'ayatollahs' which do not seem to be needed by any other art: Pluralism flourishes in film, music, painting, poetry, product design, sculpture, television, theatre, dance or whatever. Why does architecture need, and why do architects tolerate the dismal restricting pronouncements of their 'ayatollahs'?

TAVEIRA'S LATER WORK
Clearly it is the 'ayatollahs', especially those of Minimalist persuasion, who goad Taveira into work of an opposite kind. The signs were there already with Olaias and Amoreiras, stronger still in the Banco Ultramarino. Contextual as they are to Lisbon, neither Amoreiras nor the Banco have anything to do with that awkward hybrid – Frampton's Critical Regionalism. They are far too Populist for that. Taveira's brief for Pereira de Melo sought a design that was even more literal in context. He was required to retain existing facades, which he did, as a kind of scenic ruin. Kahn after all had built screen walls, new ruins as it were, around his Salk Institute and Taveira had no problems in retaining those that were there. Behind his complex shopping centre turns out to be, consciously or not, a commentary on Rossi's Cemetery windows surmounted by a blue glass cube – a fragment, as it were, of Don Carlos – held in place by a rather visible hand in stained glass of quite riotous colours. There is a blue glass cone, somewhat truncated, with a yellow frill, of the kind one finds around the neck of a cutlet and other interventions and penetrations which could not criticise more directly the bleak sterilities of Modena and so much other Minimalism; straight curtains, walled slabs, also curved ones. And then to 'frame' the site from the back as it were two, more or less classical temples were extended as towers with understated pediments. One can write, as I have, about the sheer tedium of abstract Minimalism architecture, but as Summerson suggested, towards the end of this life, criticism need not consist entirely of writing; it may come as three-dimensional forms, actual buildings, which show what is wrong with the

others. Taveira is a critic of that kind.

This is the substance of Taveira's other recent designs: his Metro Station; in, around and beneath a motorway intersection with markers at surface level between the slip roads. Including a Trade Centre with rentable rooms and a station for 50 buses. The Metro by its nature is underground but it reaches three storeys towards the light with a huge, cathedral-like space crossed by bridges. Over and around the actual Station there's the commercial centre and a shopping centre brightened, as one might expect, by all that advertising can do. A Station, after all, has a captive audience – their lives may be brightened by such things. And if they go on to buy, then so much the better. That is the purpose of such a centre.

The most serious of Taveira's later schemes is an extension to Lisbon's Palace of National Assembly. A classical building, in the Bairro Alto approached – to its central portico – by a huge flight of steps from the picturesque heart of historic Lisbon. The extension is to contain new offices, parking for deputies and so on, somewhat beyond its northern corner and linked to the palace by a tunnel. Some 30 architects competed, soon reduced to five and then to two including Taveira. A final decision is awaited.

Taveira met the highly detailed brief by designing two, slanted facade blocks like Libeskind's in Berlin, each with an inner open court and splayed on plan towards each other across a larger court. A Libeskind-like bean – containing meeting rooms – slopes across them. It starts four storeys in the air at a tower to the north like a fragment of Don Carlos and stops to the south of them. So Taveira embraces Deconstruction, which he sees, unlike Minimalism, as possessing intellectual content. Demanding decisions have to be made about exactly how the angles clash, how the fragments penetrate each other, than ever could be needed with simple geometry.

Deconstruction also permeates his Penitentiary for Dordrecht where, given Holland's enlightened prison regime there are cell-blocks of course where the inmates live, but meeting places too and places even for their entertainment. Taveira's idea was that his Prison should be 'unashamed to be a prison!'

The brief was remarkably detailed and Taveira satisfied every point by making the prison like a small town, in cross formation with rather unequal arms. His residential units are quite large open malls, at right angles to each other but widening from the crossing to their outer ends which terminate in oval access towers. These are balanced over the crossing by smaller buildings; high security in oval access towers, a rectangular gym and a somewhat distorted wedge of general accommodation. Taveira's colours are most un-prison-like; inspired, so he says, by Mondrian. There has been no decision yet on who gets to build what no doubt may be called the 'Dordrecht Hilton!'

TAVEIRA'S TRANSFORMATIONS

Taveira has been concerned over the years with – like Picasso – transfiguring the object. Pots and dishes are transformed into birds, and chairs are transformed into, well, chairs with differences. There is no distinction for Taveira between Le Corbusier's machine for sitting in and Mackintosh's chair as sculpture. It is easy for the two to be combined so a chair might sprout ears or a clubfoot, a sunburst for a back or whatever. He greatly enjoyed designing a Minimalist chair to show how hostile to the human frame it could be. For, however riotous the forms and colour Taveira uses, his chairs still have legs, backs and seats, in eminently 'sittable' positions. There is something exciting says Taveira, about producing objects which function, overlaid with a burden of art. The sculptural nature of their forms – as in some of Taveira's couches, means specific comfort for two people where an ordinary three-seater may well just enable them to sit.

As a Populist, however, it is natural that Taveira's skills be deployed by the 'mass media'; in that most accessible of forms these days: television. He is employed by Lisbon's SIC as an image-making set designer because he knows when to evoke the safety of Classicism, say for a music festival; *risqué* intimacy for a series on 'In bed with. . .' and so on.

TAVEIRA'S VIEWS ON EDUCATION

Tomás Taveira has been Dean, since 1991, of the Faculty of Architecture in the Technical University of Lisbon. As a pluralist indeed he is worried about the ways the 'ayatollahs' influence his students. Of course they read the journals like students everywhere and when all they see is elephants the Pluralism he seeks is diminished in his School.

Moreover, he worries about his School's position in a Technical University, dominated of course by engineers. He has no quarrel with them. Engineers have their ways of thinking; immensely successful in so many fields; civil electrical, mechanical and so on. But architects have different ways of thinking; part art, part psychology, part technology which is very different from any other. But it may be and is applied in the other arts of painting, sculpture, fashion, jewellery, interior design, industrial design, urban design and economics; everything to do with the performing arts including theatre, cinema and video; script writing, scenography, acting dance, music and costume design. These share certain ways of thinking which make them, for Taveira, aspects of architecture. So his dream of course is for a University of Architecture where creativity, social responsibility and technical skills are taught, in thorough integration. Architecture unifies the arts, indeed uses painting and sculpture. But theatre unifies too performance of any kind. Even inferior components; poor book, banal music, good costumes perhaps and set design may, in production and performance, establish a whole far greater than the sum of its parts, as in musicals such as *Evita*, *Phantom of the Opera*, *Miss Saigon* and so on.

Taveira's breadth of approach is in absolute contrast to say Mies', at IIT, where the Master knew best and others had to conform. The pluralist Taveira encourages in his School Minimalism, Classicism, Deconstruction; his own brand of form that follows fun and so on. For architecture to survive – as art, as science or whatever – we need figures like Taveira to challenge, even ridicule, the more solemn of established values; to keep Fundamentalists at bay. Taveira reminds us – and many seem to need reminding – that form, following function – may also be fun!

REFERENCES

Gropius W, *The Scope of Total Architecture,* Allen and Unwin, London, 1956

Peter J (Rec and ed), *Conversations Regarding the Future of Architecture* (Long Playing Record) Reynolds Metal Company, Louisville, Kentucky, 1956

Pevsner N, *Pioneers of the Modern Movement,* Faber and Faber, London, 1936; new edition, Museum of Modern Art, New York, 1949; revised and partly rewritten, Penguin Books, Harmondsworth, 1960

Frampton K, *Modern Architecture and the Critical Present*, AD Profile 42, Academy Editions, London, 1982

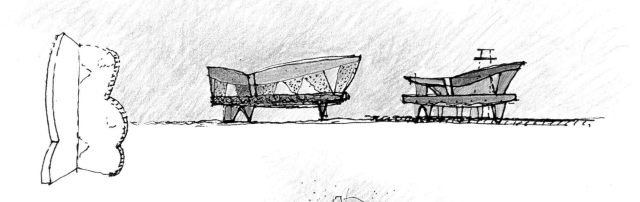

TOMÁS TAVEIRA IMAGINATION VERSUS FUNDAMENTALISM

A wide group of tendencies exists in contemporary architecture which has been obscured by the excessive disposition to value everything that is tradition: modern, neo-rationalist, Aaltian and Le Corbusian architectural tradition.

Whatever efforts Post-Modernism has achieved in reintroducing new ideas and new imaginations into the architectonic world, these have been both reviled and largely attacked and its members put aside totally from the international scene, particularly from the most respected publications.

There are 'grunge', minimalistic, fundamentalist, almost religious fashions concerning modern architecture's greatest moments of the fifties which are promoted widely, either through books or architecture magazines from the main publishing houses. This is so much the case that one may actually say that neither the publishers nor a single architecture critic dare pronounce any word not giving support to anything which presents itself as being varied.

Due to the weight and influence of architects such as Renzo Piano and Norman Foster in politics, culture and the business world, it would be unwise to silence them; it is only because of its uncommon and 'impressive' details and structures, as well as its paraphernalia that the so-called High-Tech architecture is given any coverage. According to theoreticians of the same calibre as those mentioned above, any transformation that takes place in an historic city must be done in a minimal way with total respect for the past; this of course does not take into account that historical forms at their time of creation were totally new and in some cases revolutionary.

Colours are now understood as false and the return to white (and to black) demands that one accepts man as Daltonian or at least that one accepts that architecture cannot have colour any more! Any 'alteration' concerning the *modus operandi* of the so called neo-rationalist traditional architecture is always considered as an 'aberration', a 'deviation' from the cosmic perfection as it is understood by this aesthetic expression.

In order to attain an architect/thinker status it is necessary, as well as wise, that in the current cultural stage everyone accepts this rule, without which one would become both a show-off with an aggressive tendency, unwise and closed as well as inartistic and unenlightened; whoever does not use the memory strategy is harebrained and if not 'neo-' lacks architectonic sensitiveness.

In architecture, everything which proceeds from beauty is meant to have derived from the 'simple'; from the 'immediate'; from the 'white'; from both *déjà vu* and *memoire*. Based upon deep research it is intended that the existence of a theoretic body be evident, and that there will be an inherent rationality to a specific architectural language which will remain predetermined forever, and by extension will never change.

Everything now seems to be a return to Bauhaus through a redefinition of Alvar Aalto's works without any concerns (or doubts). This meditation upon the Post-Modern may be seen as the trivialisation and errors of some modern movements.

It would appear that the 'historical forms' and their integration into architecture are not what represents the Post-Modern Movement's basic stance; it seems that Post-Modernism hasn't made the slightest criticism; it has not fathomed out what was the Modern Movement, nor has it concluded that this one was either recopied (as happens today) or that it would simply be swallowed; and that is manifestedly different from an Alvar Aalto or a Mies van der Rohe detailed copy!

Today it is pertinent to ask: What is the truthful Post-Modern project? Is it Le Corbusier? Is it Alvar Aalto? Is it Rossi? Is it the Critical Regionalism of Kenneth Frampton?

Does the unmimeticised cult manner integration of the idea in the historical site also make part of the revisited modern world culture or is it a Post-Modern conquest? Has the recovery of the vernacular effectively been a modern stance? Is this the case in which all problematic architecture goes inevitably through the historic city rehabilitation task?

If one intends it to be like this, one has then to ask if either neo-rationalist and Critical Regionalism do actually know how to settle the difference between projecting:
– under the context influence
– under the *genius loci* influence
– under the contrast influence
– under the analogy coin?

In the anti-context euphoria climax at the CIAM IV (1933), the Athens declaration stated that: 'The utilisation of past styles in a new construction, built in an historical site with aesthetic pretences serviceably copying the past, has nasty consequences which is to condemn oneself to deception'.

Though these ideas might paradoxically have been spread by Le Corbusier – whom whether one likes it or not is still neo-rationalism's greatest inspiration as well as its father – they were left out in the cold and this rationalist vanguard which intended a total city revitalisation was severely criticised. It still seems today that these ideas don't deserve to be condemned.

As the neo-rationalists are reacting against both Aalto and Corbusier, it seems even more paradoxical to be admitting that *the city is built to the eternal* and that there is no place for a contemporary radical architectural language with an interference which was influenced by either sculpture, painting and Post-Modernism, as well as by both cinema and television.

At the end of this century the dialectic tension between modernity, cultural anthropology and history must remain as a warranty for the intellectual debate to justify that the *historic shapes* repetition has to be taken with logical purposes. All arguments are valid today and taking the view that architecture is not workmanship design it follows therefore that history never repeats. On the other hand, all neo-rationalists seem to be forgetting that if there is anything which *in art* isn't determined by anyone/thing, it is precisely that: logic.

In determining a new entitlement with regard to the city, one always talks about the 'Left European Interference'. In this, one includes the historic shapes revitalisation. But this Left seems to be in the heart of a tremendous mixing-up and even the neo-fundamentalists are confronted with a considerable amount of hard work, trying to be both coherent and consistent; whereas in this quest for consistency, interferences appear, such as those which are both occurring, or have occurred, in either Lisbon (Chiado) and Berlin's city centre.

Since both Rossi's and Eisenman's projects have nothing to do with their context, everything becomes acceptable in Berlin; whereas in Lisbon it is said that Chiado is becoming a masterpiece just because it comes directly from its context.

Is this the case in which what effectively matters is that protection is to be given to architects who are divulging neo-rationalist architecture? However, in aiming to be giving *protection* to just one single idea while silencing all others, are we not actually falling within a neo-totalitarian fascist radicalism?

Is this the case in which some sort of Aryan cleaning up stance is enveloping the architectonic criticism against whatever reminds it of something different from neo-rationalism?

Isn't this a rehabilitation culture syndrome from which we are suffering? Aren't we entitled to the right of building up our own city? And to the right of building up an *entirely new* city?

Doesn't this stance imply a much higher imagination quality than environmental pre-existing maintenance and neo-rationalism? Could Sant'Elia not have been correct when he wrote in the *Futuristic Architecture Manifesto*, Milan, 1914: 'The houses shall remain for even less than us. Each generation is entitled to build its own city'?

Like many architects I think that my architecture is actually being silenced in several specialised magazines, both in the USA and Europe, since there is a total subduing of actual criticism towards the above ideas.

But this subduing also exists at the architecture school level, wherein one learns the good Rossian way of how to make just one single project, only one type of interference; the education is enfeebled and neo-mediocre. This is far more serious.

In spite of all adversities I believe that with a renewal of ideas a new criticism emerges. In the last two decades under the neo-rationalists' banner, nothing of what was done has any consistency whatsoever, apart from a constructive quality which is not the same as art work, nor stands for imagination. That is why I still fathom an architecture, which although in possession of roots which vaguely recall the past, is also committed towards the future. What makes it truly radical against the opinions of those who only want to see within it the revisited past, is that it is exciting and lively, vibrant and colourful. Frankly, I think that both new dialectics and new imaginations can be democratically returned to the pages of both publishing houses and magazines.

VALENTIM DE CARVALHO RECORD SHOP

This building exhibits clear historicist influences. In plan it resembles a replica of St Peter's in Rome, whilst its spatial structure is reminiscent of the poetic baroque. The decoration within the shop was treated as an integral work of art where architecture, painting, sculpture and poetry co-exist; Sa Nogueira was the painter and Herberto Helder the poet that gave inspiration.
(*Cascais, Portugal 1969-70*)

Ground floor plan; PAGE 18: Section and front elevation; PAGE 19: Side elevation

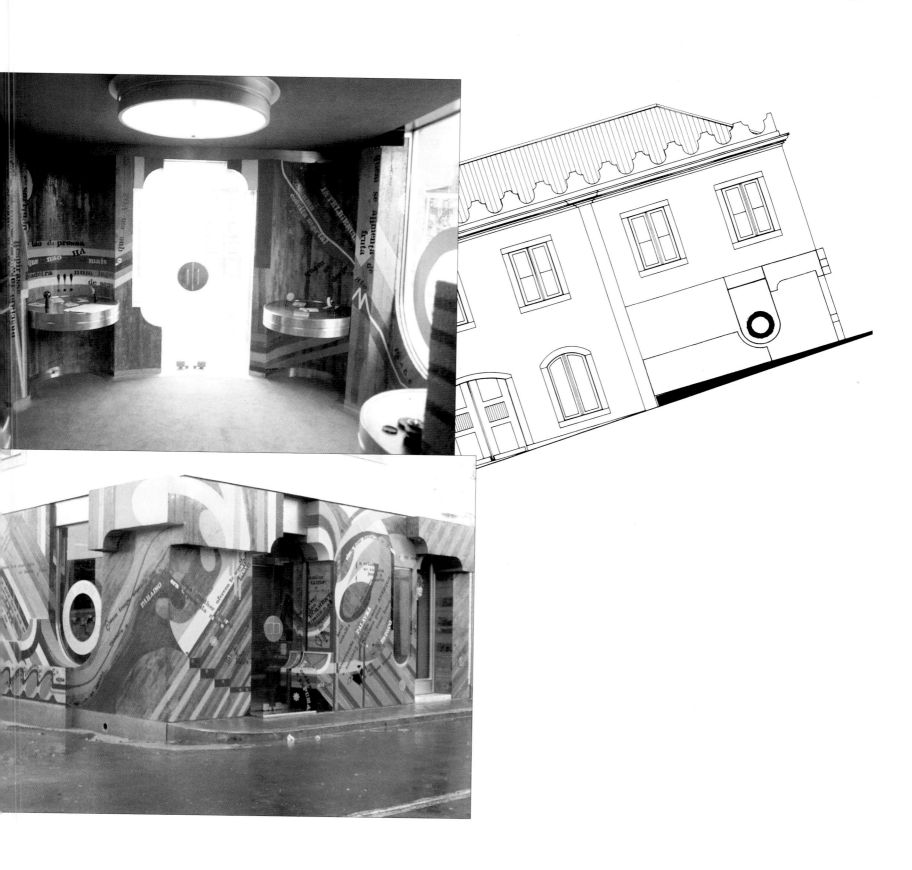

For this factory the poetic idea was more or less the same as that applied to the record shop, at least as far as the influence of history on the design was concerned. But inspiration was also found in another period of artistic creation, that of Roman and Gothic architecture, particularly in Lisbon's oldest Cathedral (built in the 13th century). The original project was intended to be of a larger scale, but today it still lacks the administration building and social and leisure area. (*Paço d'Arcos, Portugal, 1968-70*)

Second floor plan; PAGE 23: Axonometric

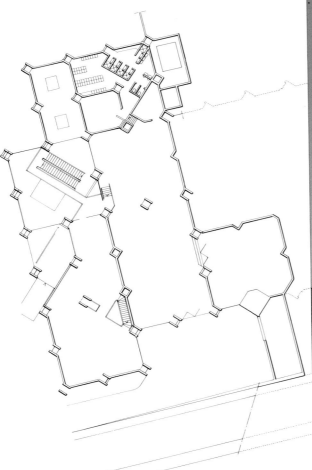

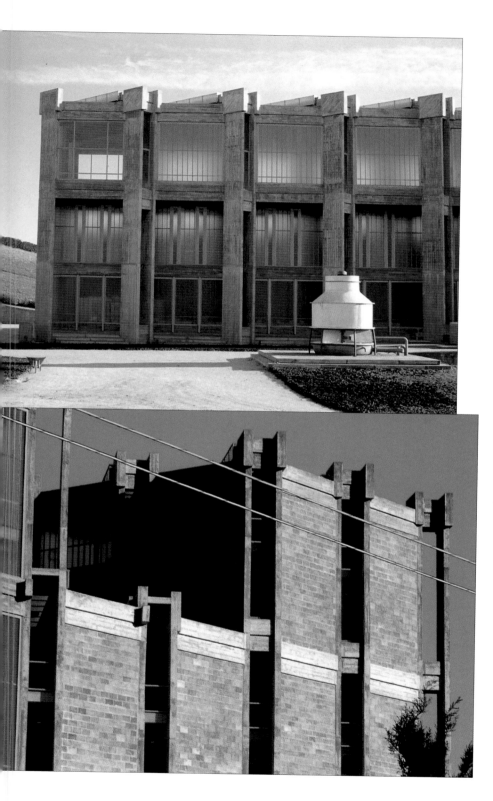

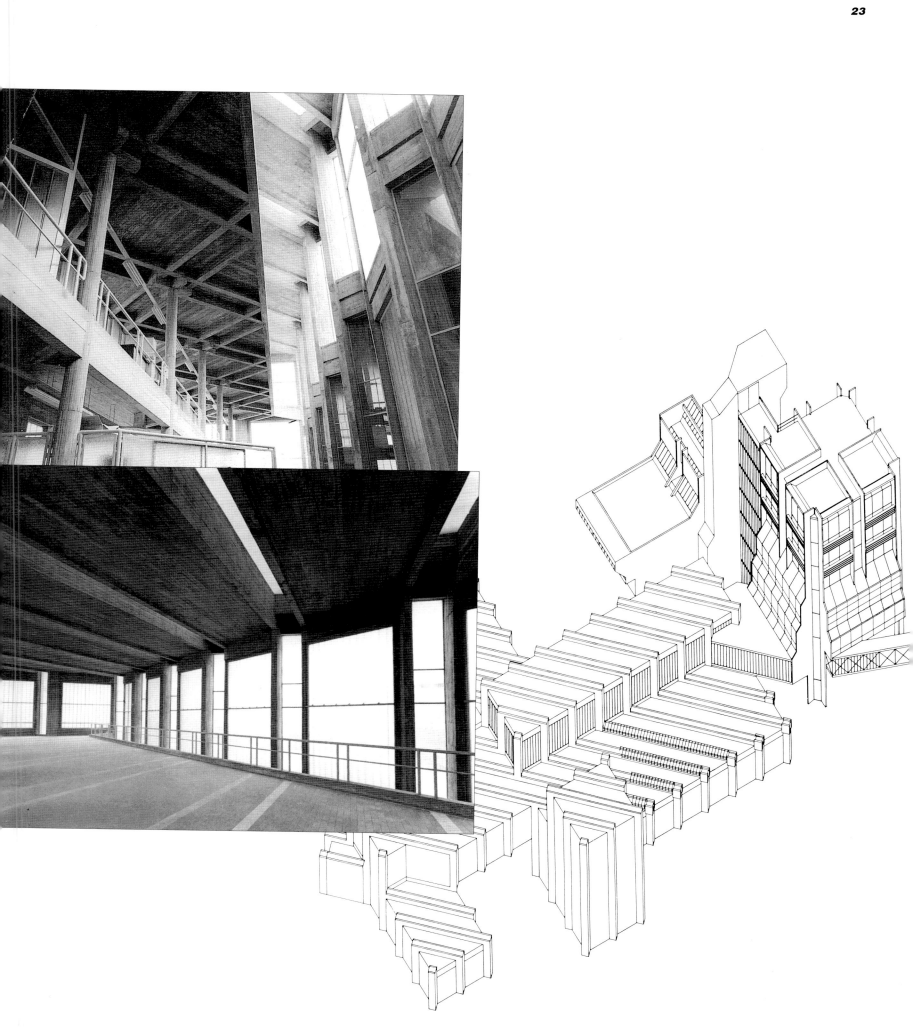

CHELAS SOCIAL HOUSING COMPLEX

This low-cost, high-density housing was designed for the most impoverished area of West Lisbon. It was the result of a competition organised by Lisbon Council. The project is made up of double apartments and galleries. Its design is a compromise between Muslim architecture, cosmopolitan and modern influences which gives it a sense of neo-Realism. It was also the first instance of Arabic influence on the works. The *International Herald Tribune* concluded that the people living there were happy with the flats. (*Lisbon, Portugal, 1975-78*)

East elevation of tower block; PAGE 25: North-west elevation and fifth floor plan of block type A; PAGE 26: Site plan

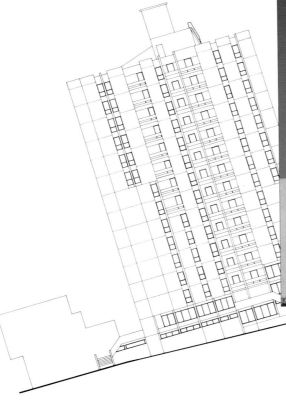

DON CARLOS I BUILDING

This building was designed in 1973, and was intended to have been built in steel. It was designed to relate to the industrial landscape where it is situated, and to be articulated with the image of the River Tagus frontage. This intention was not accomplished because the political revolution of 1974 altered the economic conditions. As a result, the building had to be constructed in concrete. However, the image created is similar to the original conception. (*Lisbon, Portugal, 1973-83*)

North and south elevations; PAGE 29: Ground and typical floor plans; PAGE 30: West elevation

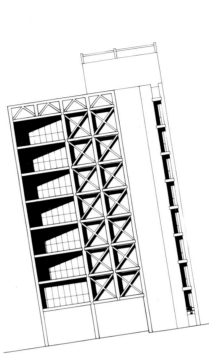

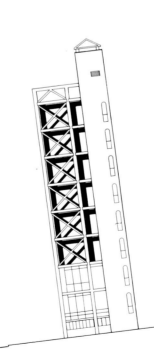

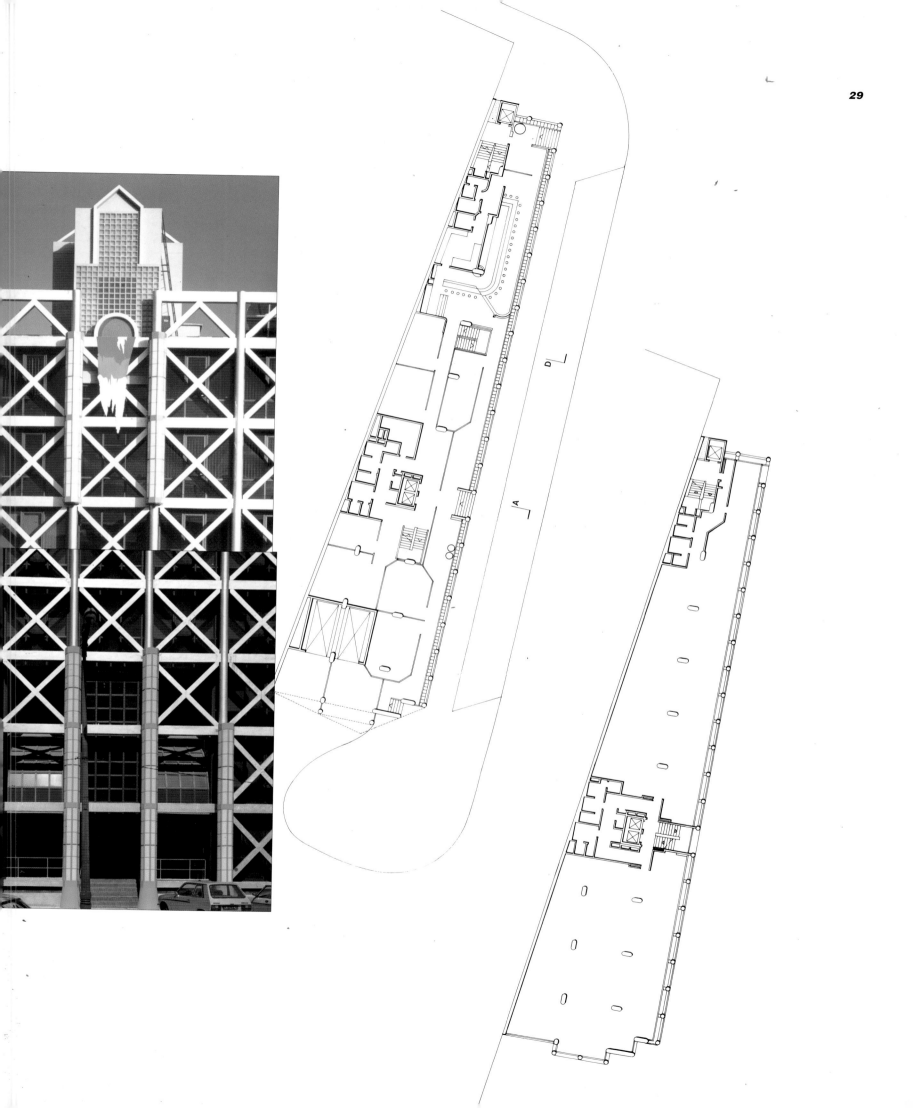

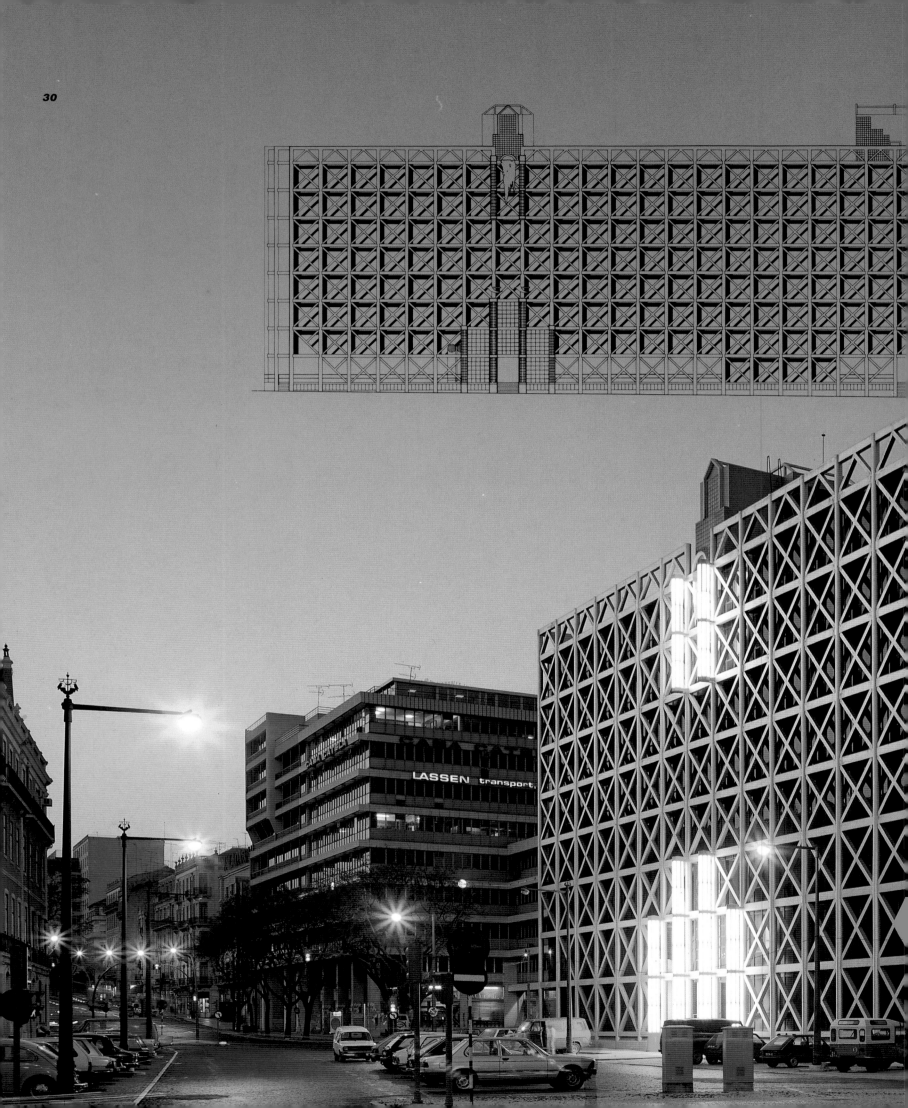

SATELLITE OFFICE BUILDING

The aesthetic image of this building suffered many changes at project stage, because it was designed in the late-Modern era and finished amidst the throws of the Post-Modern debate. As a result, the design was a compromise; midway between the neo-classical, late-Modern and Pop. Today the building is viewed as a first attempt at reaching the Post-Modern solution. (*Lisbon, Portugal, 1972-82*)

Ground floor plan; PAGE 33: Cross section

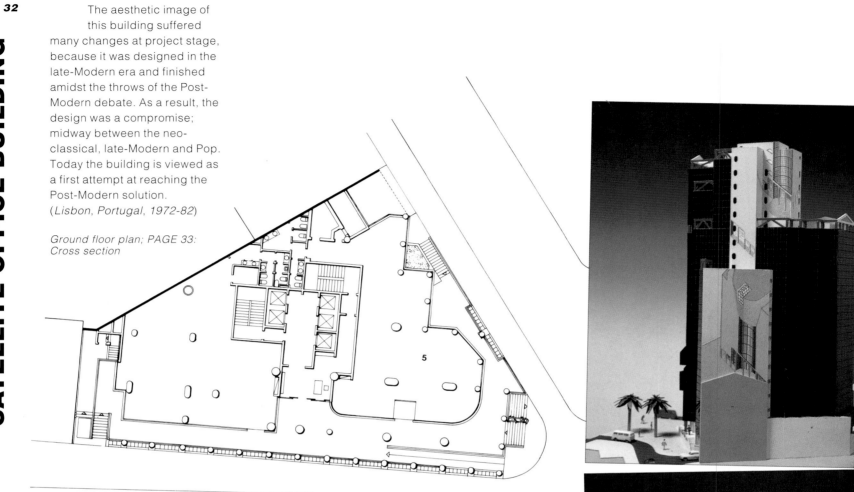

AMOREIRAS TOWER COMPLEX

This group of buildings consists of housing (luxury flats), offices and a shopping mall. It is one of the largest private urban complexes in Portugal. Perhaps the most accomplished Post-Modern work yet constructed, it most clearly sets out the poetic constraints that define Post-Modernism. These constraints include the cultural anthropology of the place, (ie Lisbon), reference to the medieval and Muslim culture, the use of historic references (neo-classicism), the use of colour and ornamentation and a single democratic idea of monumentality and surprise which Portuguese architecture was not alone in having lost. (*Lisbon, Portugal, 1980-86*)

North-west and south-west elevations; PAGE 37: Axonometric; PAGE 38: 15th floor plan of Tower II; PAGE 39: 14th floor plan of Tower I; PAGE 41: Sections of Tower I and Tower II; PAGE 44: Section of housing; PAGE 45: Typical floor plan of housing

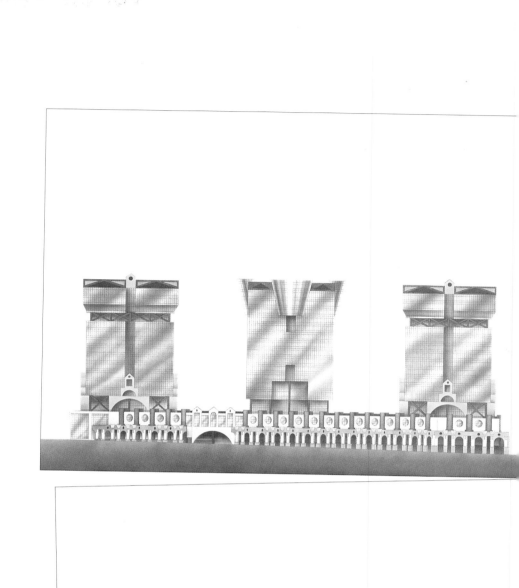

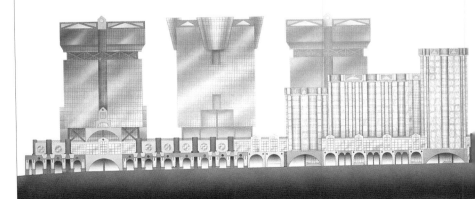

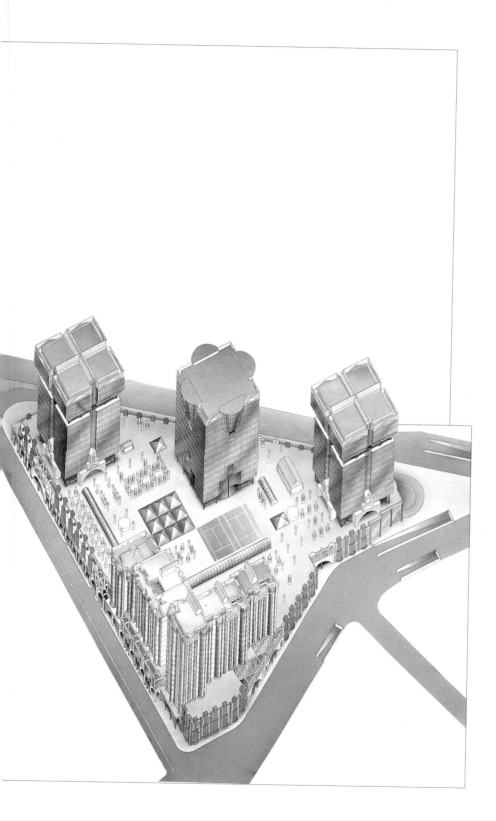

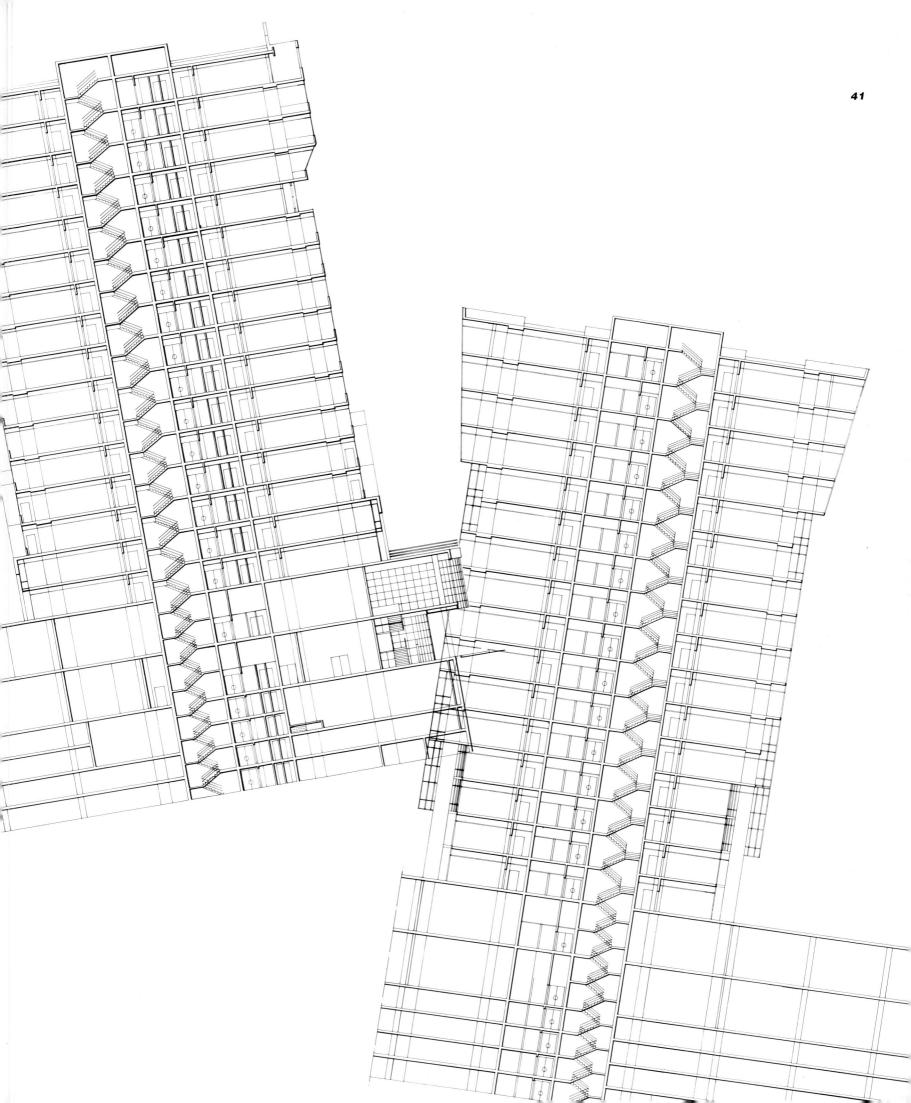

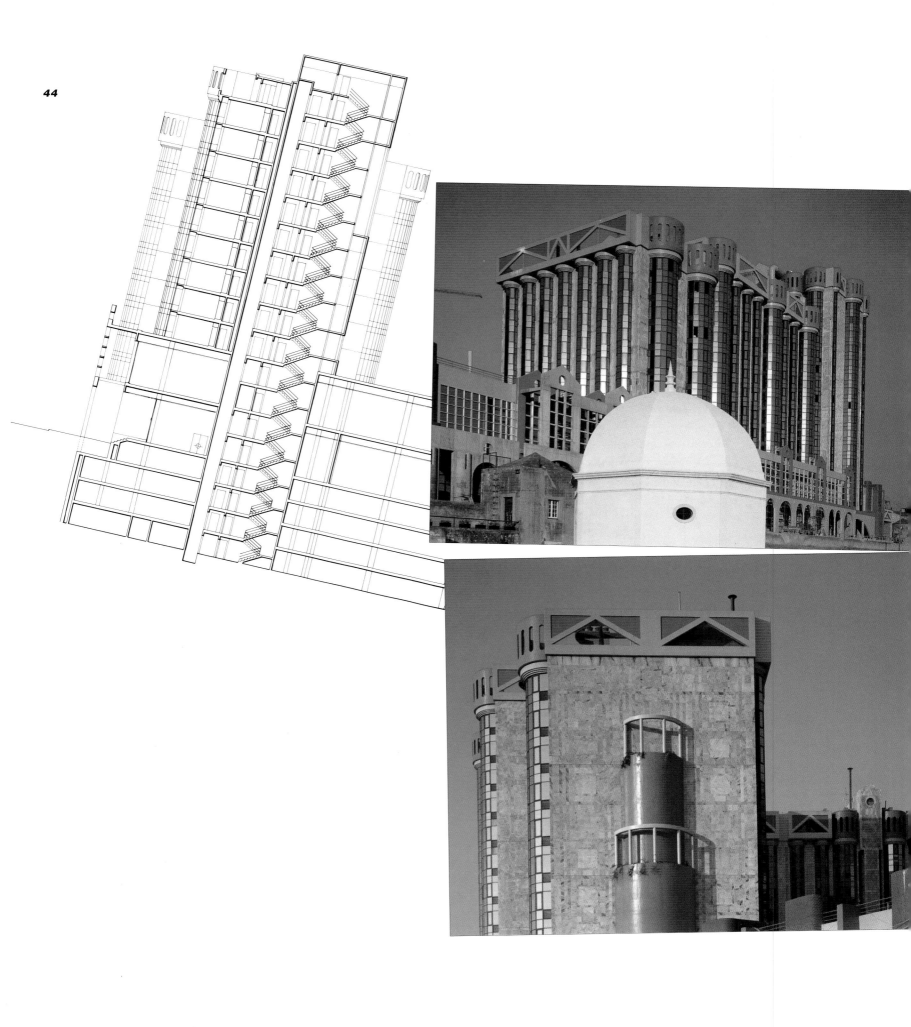

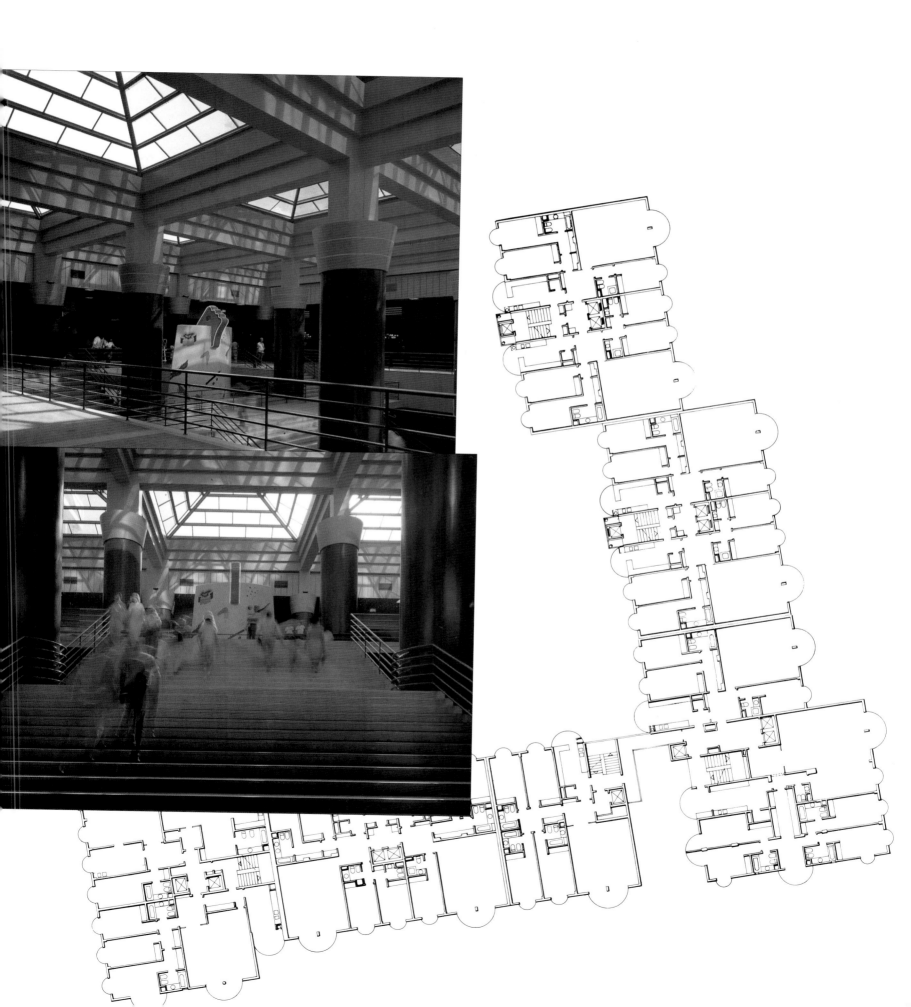

This is the largest bank headquarters built in Lisbon so far. It is a self-contained unit including all the various functions usually found in a bank with social facilities for its employees. It covers 66,000 square metres and accommodates 680 people. The building is sited on the fringe of an area of Lisbon developed in the 1940s; but the immediate location of the buildings is anonymous, lacking a special cultural quality.

However, two buildings exist in the vicinity which are very much part of Portuguese culture: one is the Fatima Church (built in the 40s) and the other is the bullring built at the beginning of this century. Both of them influenced the design in different ways. The church is in the style of late Portuguese Modernism (architecture produced under the influence of Salazar's Minister of Culture and Propaganda). The bullring represents one of the best examples of the influence of Maghreb Architecture. Seven centuries of Arabic presence in the Iberian Peninsula have left a strong impression on Portuguese culture.
(*Lisbon, Portugal, 1983-89*)

PAGE 49: Axonometric; PAGE 54: East elevation and ground floor plan; PAGE 55: North elevation and third floor plan

INTERNATIONAL TRIBUNAL FOR MARITIME LAW

This was for a competition organised by the United Nations comprising new buildings for the International Tribunal for Maritime Law, as stipulated by the United Nations Convention on Maritime Law. The competition was open to a limited number of well-known international architects including OM Ungers, Rafael Moneo, Gino Valle, Jean Nouvel and Tadao Ando. The jury stated: 'This entry may be a serious attempt to win the competition. It is certainly an articulate statement about the art of architecture. It is radical in the sense that its forms are in conflict with those of the current international establishment. It is not however anti-architectural, but shows a love for the art and can be considered a poetic statement in a time when we are sometimes afraid of poetry. It is worthy of inclusion as a statement about architecture by an architect and in the language of the art.'

This 'fragmented building' is the result of an aesthetic or even poetic option, that seems to be adapted, even artistically, to creating an architectural object. (*Hamburg, West Germany, 1989*)

Ground floor plan and south-east elevation; PAGES 58-59: First floor plan and north-east elevation; PAGES 60-61: Axonometric and north-west elevation; PAGES 62-63: Section A-A, section B-B and south-west elevation

BELEM CULTURAL CENTRE

The practice's idea was an affirmation of refusal of the rationalist architecture which has invaded the Portuguese architectural scenery. In order to be an intellectual and reputed architect in Portugal nowadays, one has to be a neo-rationalist, to copy old modern movement masters and to design everything in 'squares'!

The idea here is different in that architecture must answer all the intellectual and sensitive dimensions of man. Architecture must be a kind of music which has its own basic scale with millions of notes. Architecture must fulfil the imagination of children and old people; it must be affirmative and be related to its site, to the anthropological culture and history, which in this particular case is the Lisbon one. (*Lisbon, Portugal, 1988*)

Design sketches and axonometric; PAGES 66-67: Site plan

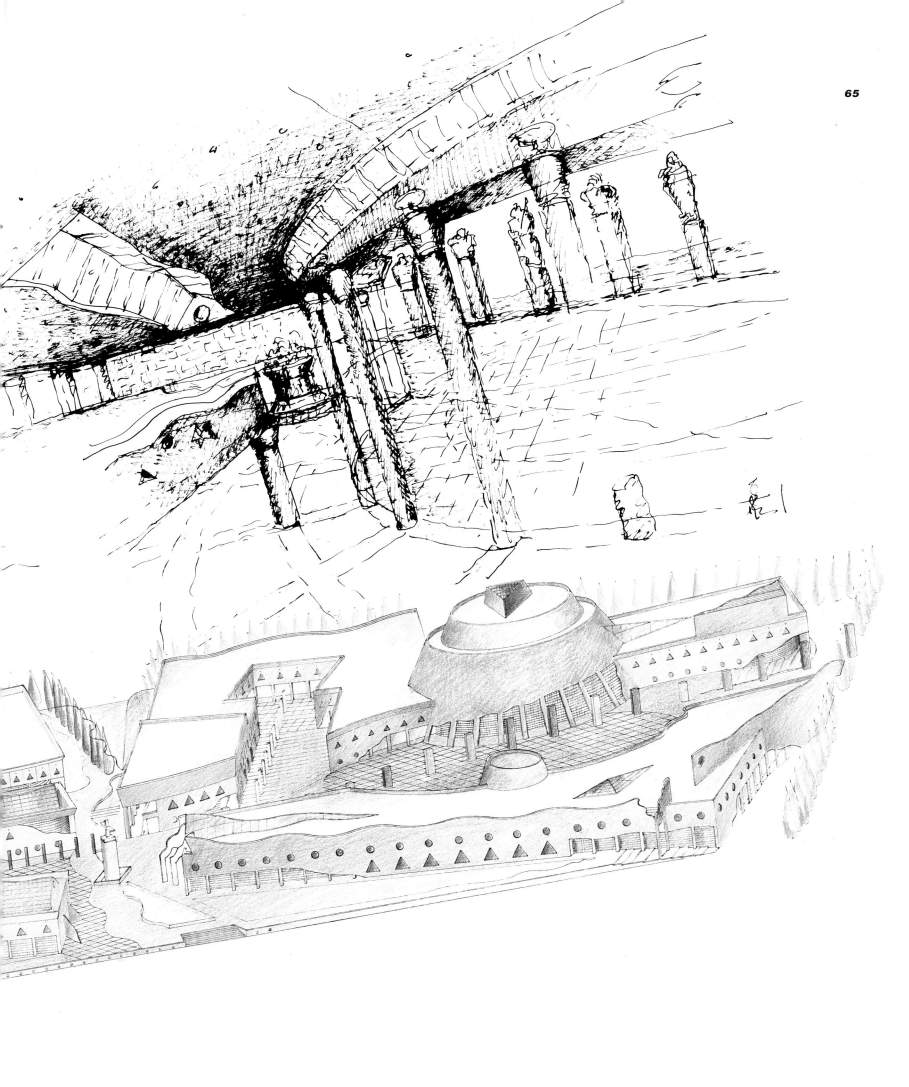

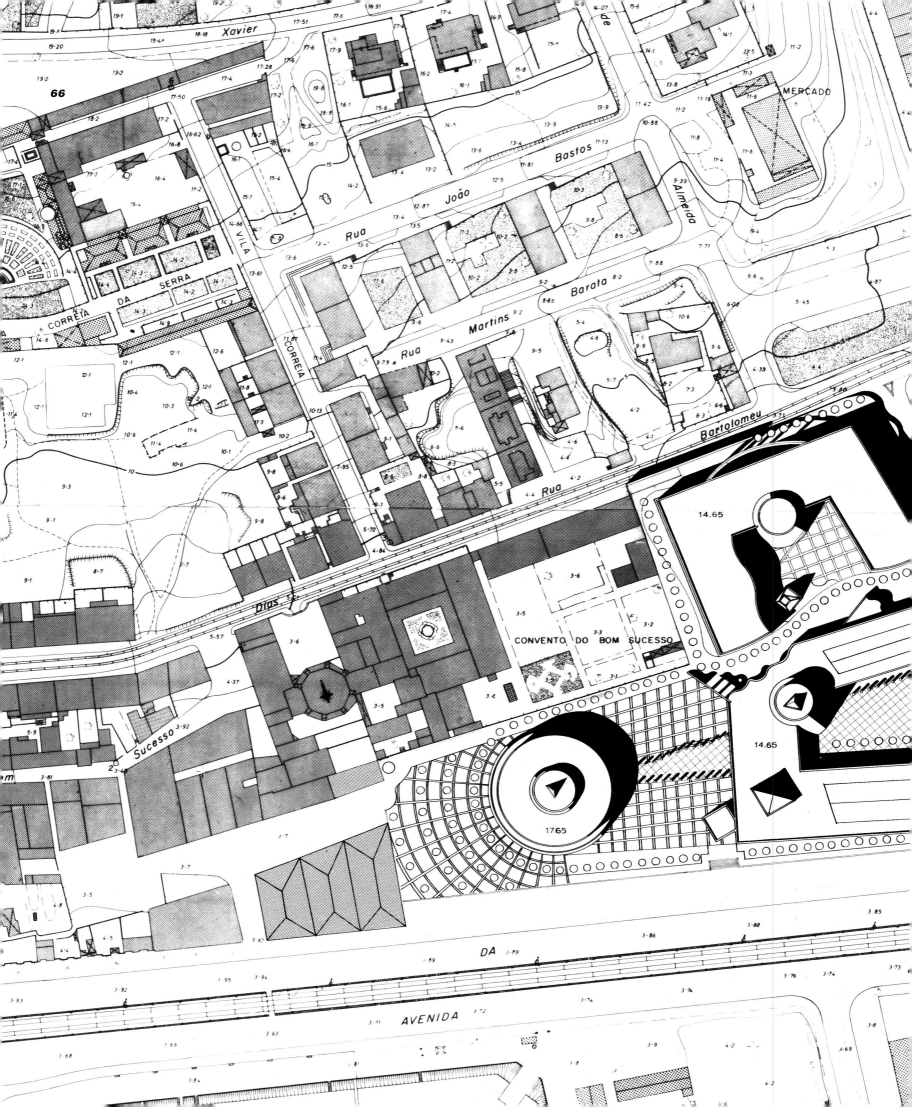

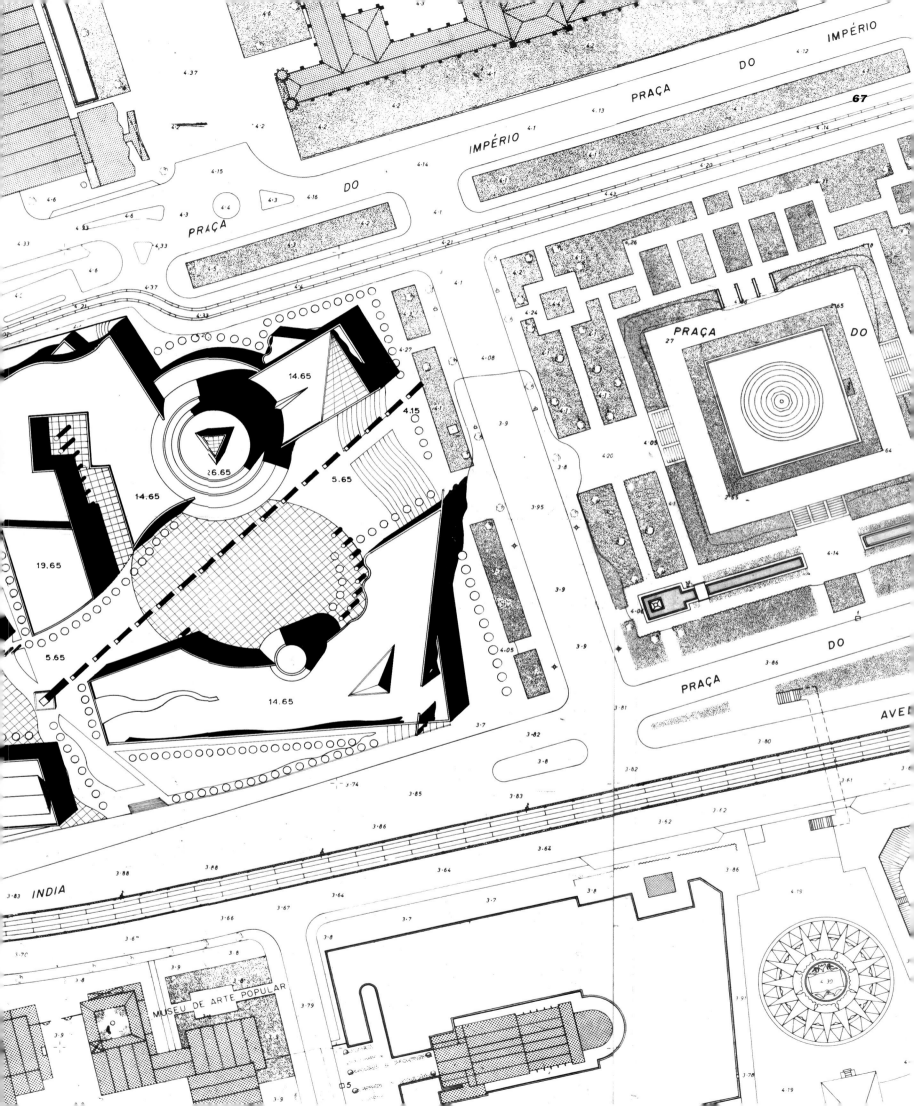

FONTES PEREIRA DE MELO BUILDING

This was intended to be a building thought of and designed in the classical way; that is, built along the streets which surround the piece of land where it would be erected.

After several months of discussion with the Lisbon Council, it was convinced to accept, 'a kind of explosion of a building (into) four', which were all in conjunction and acted as if in a non-classical architectural ballet.

The practice decided to maintain the facade of the existing building as a scenic ruin and to build up the other four on a podium dedicated to a very small shopping centre, with direct illumination via a canopy.

The area where this small complex is to be built is located in the centre of Lisbon with one side facing the major Avenida Fontes de Melo, while the other side faces a private garden.

The forms of the four buildings are reminders of the different kinds of rationalism that exist; this complex is acting against that due to the fact that it is wholly informal and non constructed. (*Lisbon, Portugal, 1993*)

Front elevation; PAGES 70-71: Side elevations; PAGES 72-73: Ground floor and seventh floor plans; PAGES 74-75: Cross section

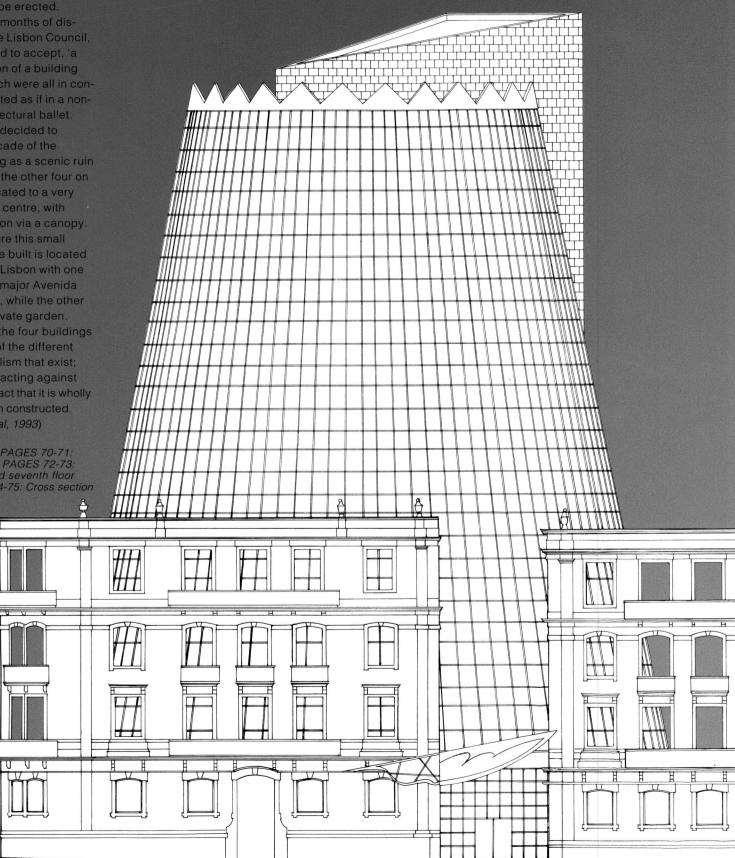

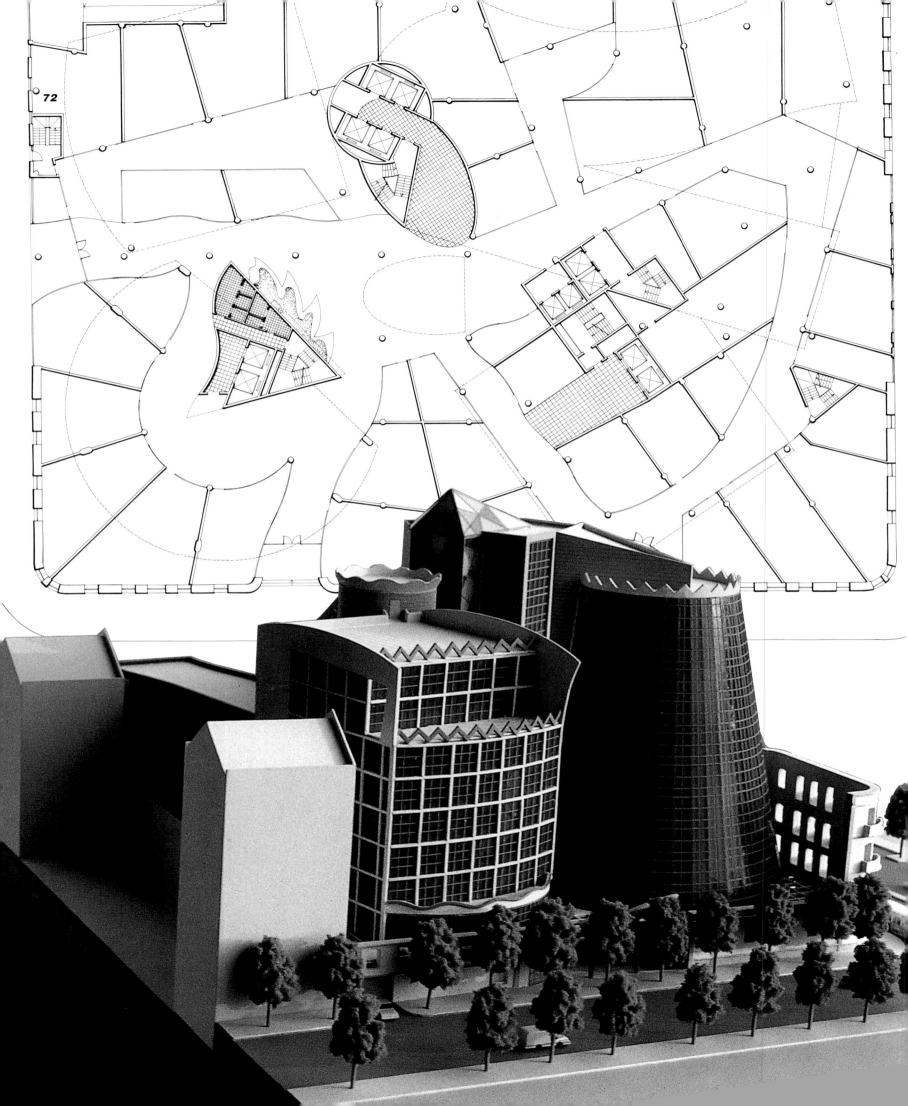

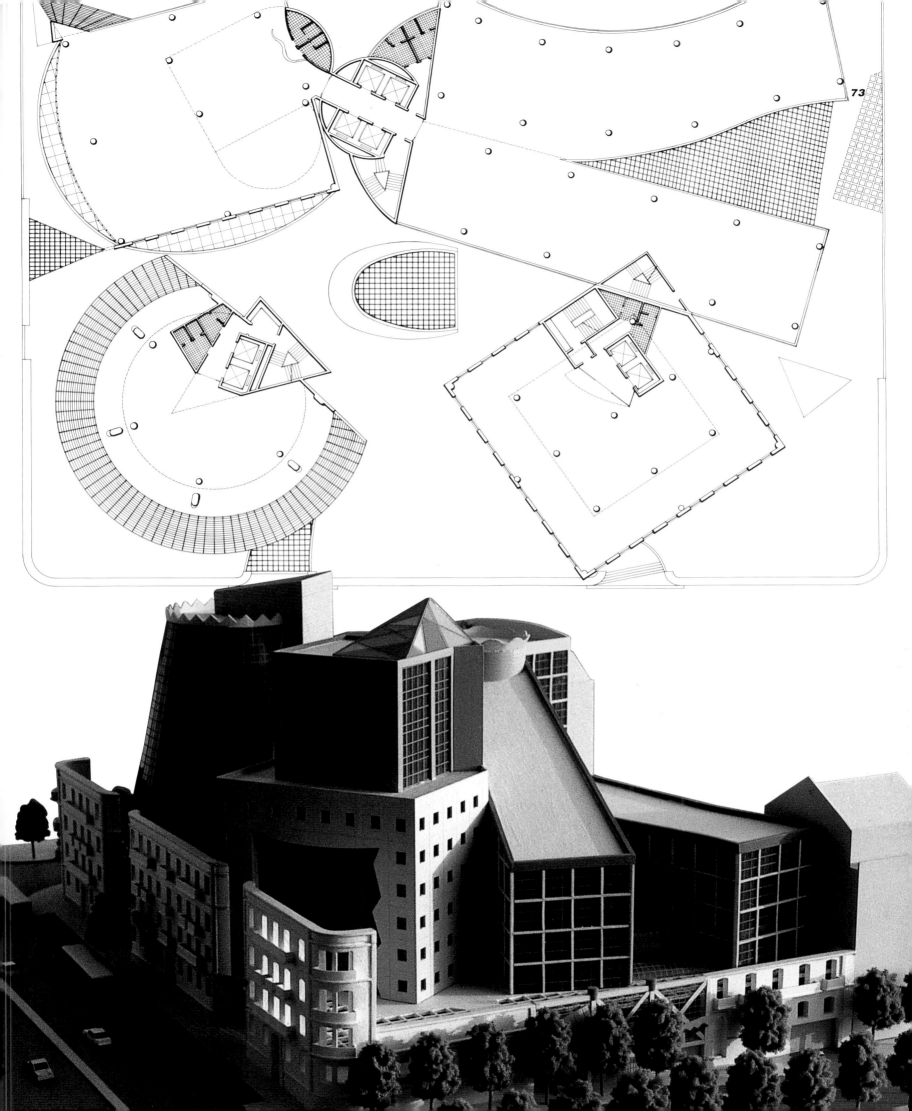

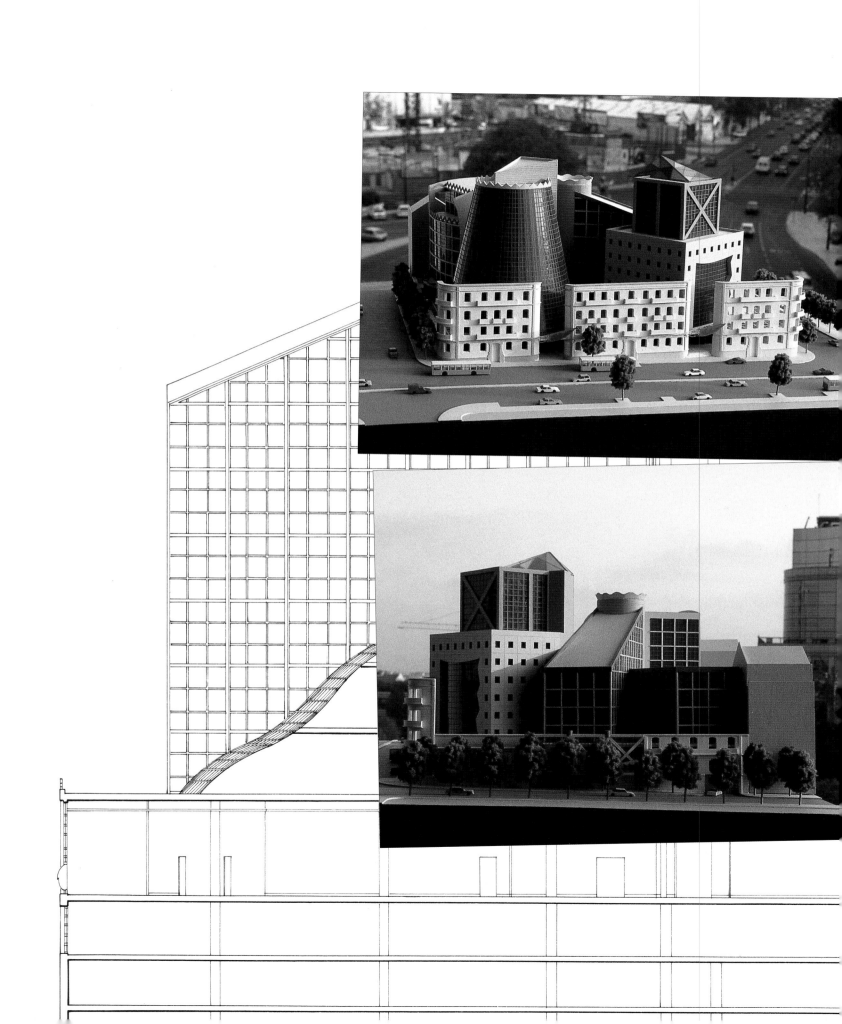

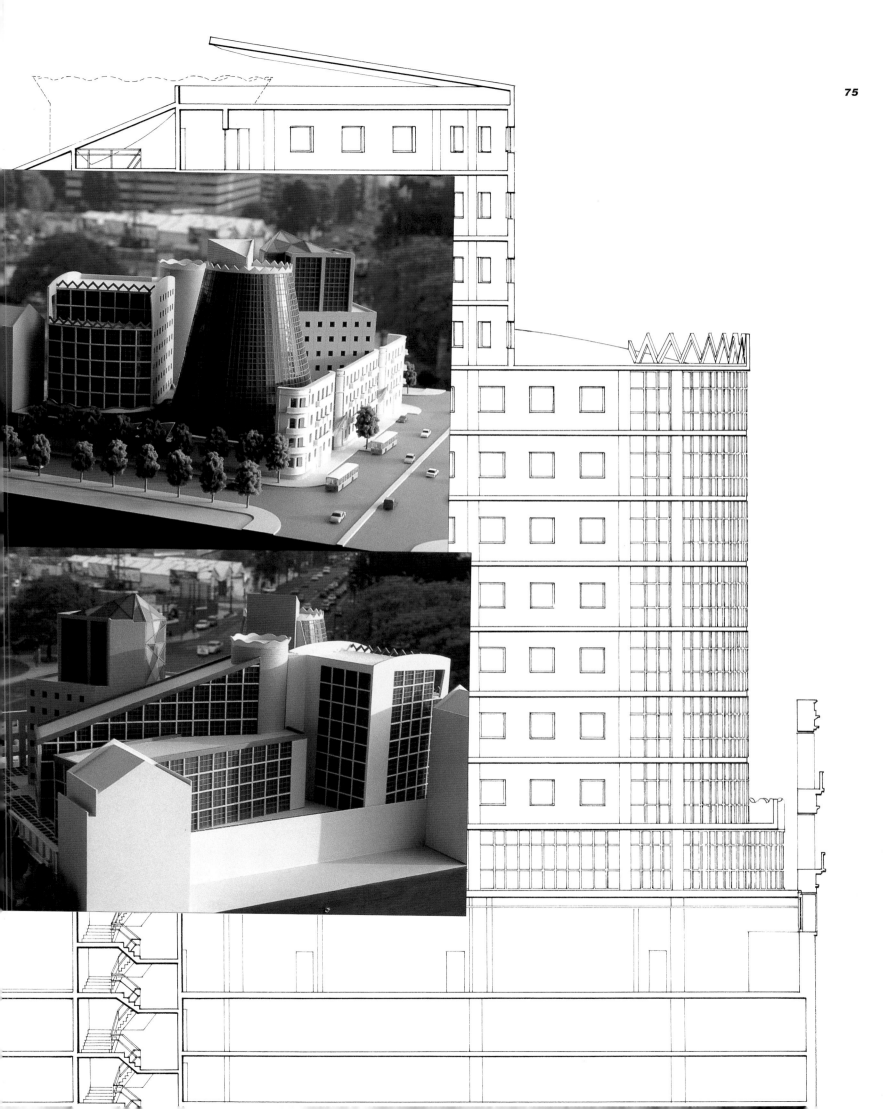

PORTUGUESE PARLIAMENT BUILDING

This was a competition in which approximately 30 Portuguese architects were invited to participate. There were two phases in the second stage of the competition in which only four other architects were selected.

The programme for the competition brief involved offices and parking spaces for the deputies due to the fact that the new building was supposed to be merely an extension of the old one with which it would be linked by a tunnel.

The Lisbon area, where the construction is integrated, is very old and while not especially characteristic, it is extremely beautiful.

For the intervention two non-perpendicular blocks were chosen crossed by a 'bridge' full of conference rooms. This is one of the practice's ideas of 'deconstruction' – that is, a deconstruction based not only on forms, but based on the excitement of colours, materials and figurative affirmation of the building.

One of the limitations of the design was in the garden of the Prime Minister's House which is located just behind the site; no windows were allowed to open onto the garden nor was the design allowed to exceed five storeys.

(*Lisbon, Portugal, 1992*)

PAGES 78-79: Ground floor plan and front elevation; PAGES 80-81: Detail of front elevation; PAGES 82-83: Third floor plan, side elevation and cross section; PAGES 86-87: Cross sections; PAGES 88-89: Axonometric; PAGES 90-91: Longitudinal section

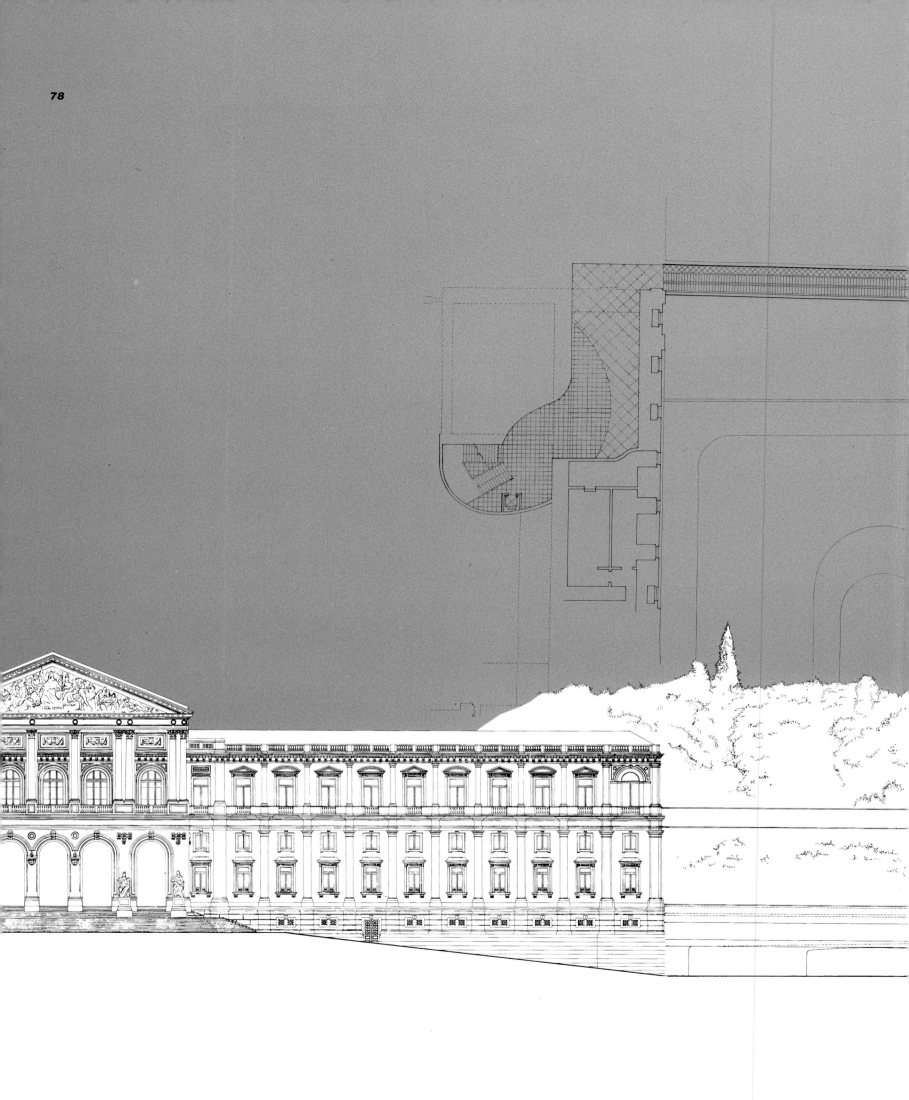

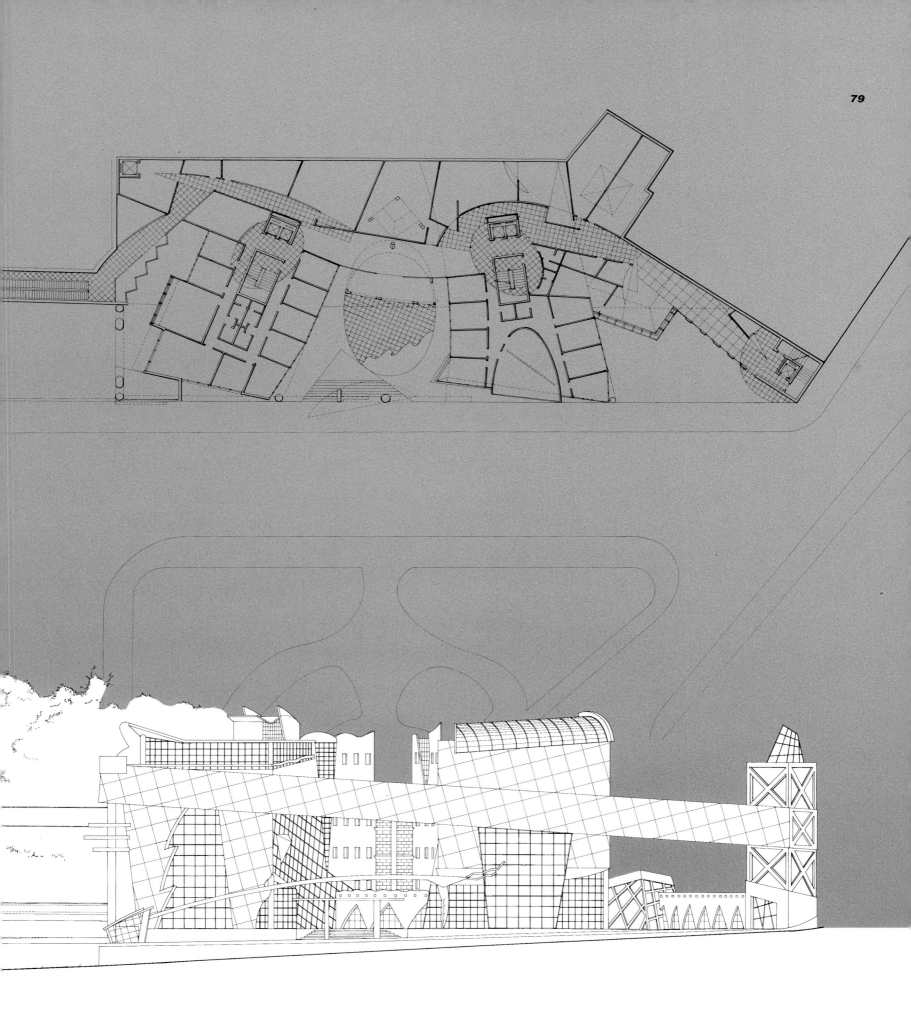

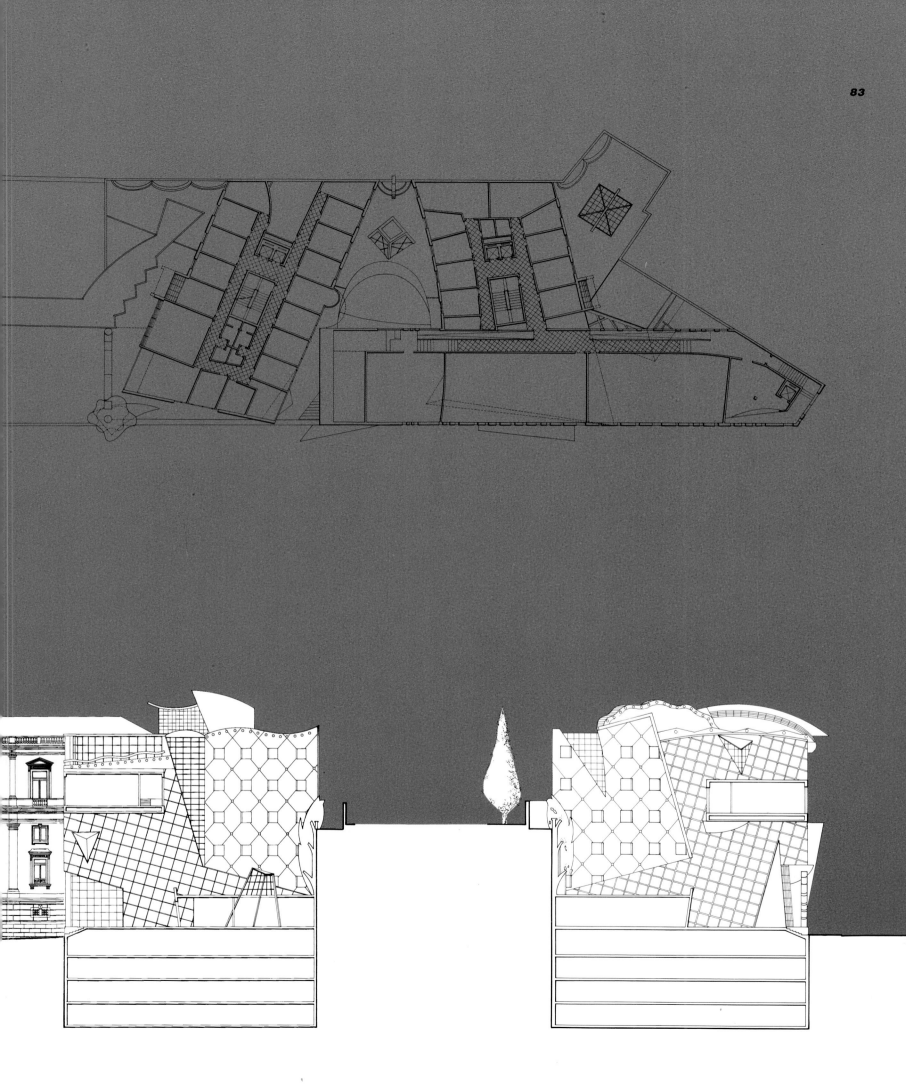

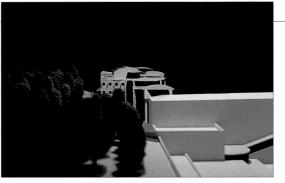

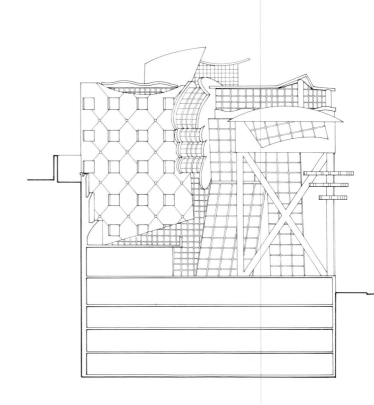

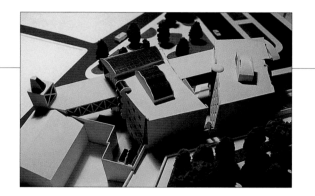

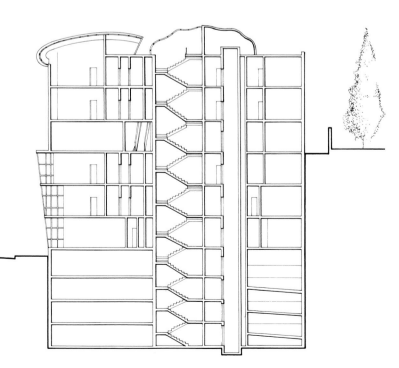

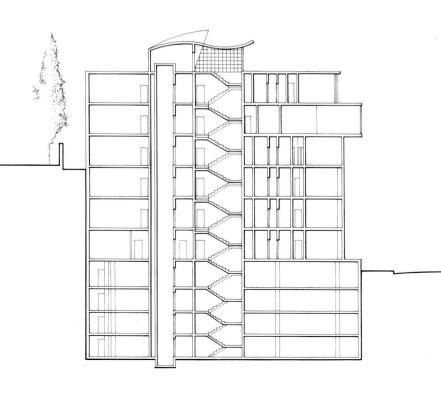

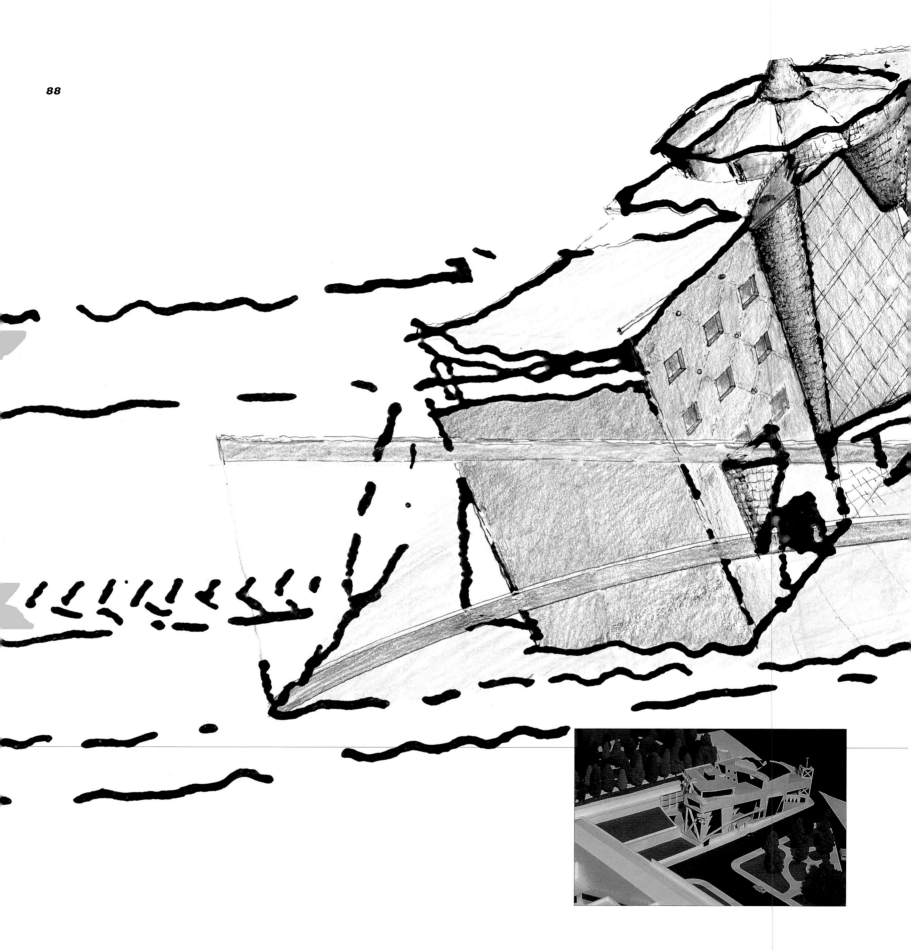

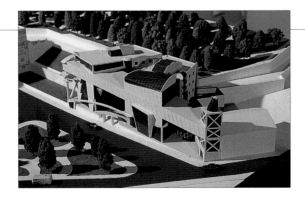

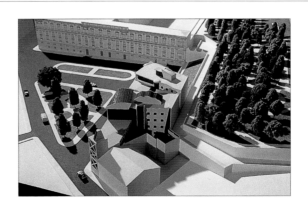

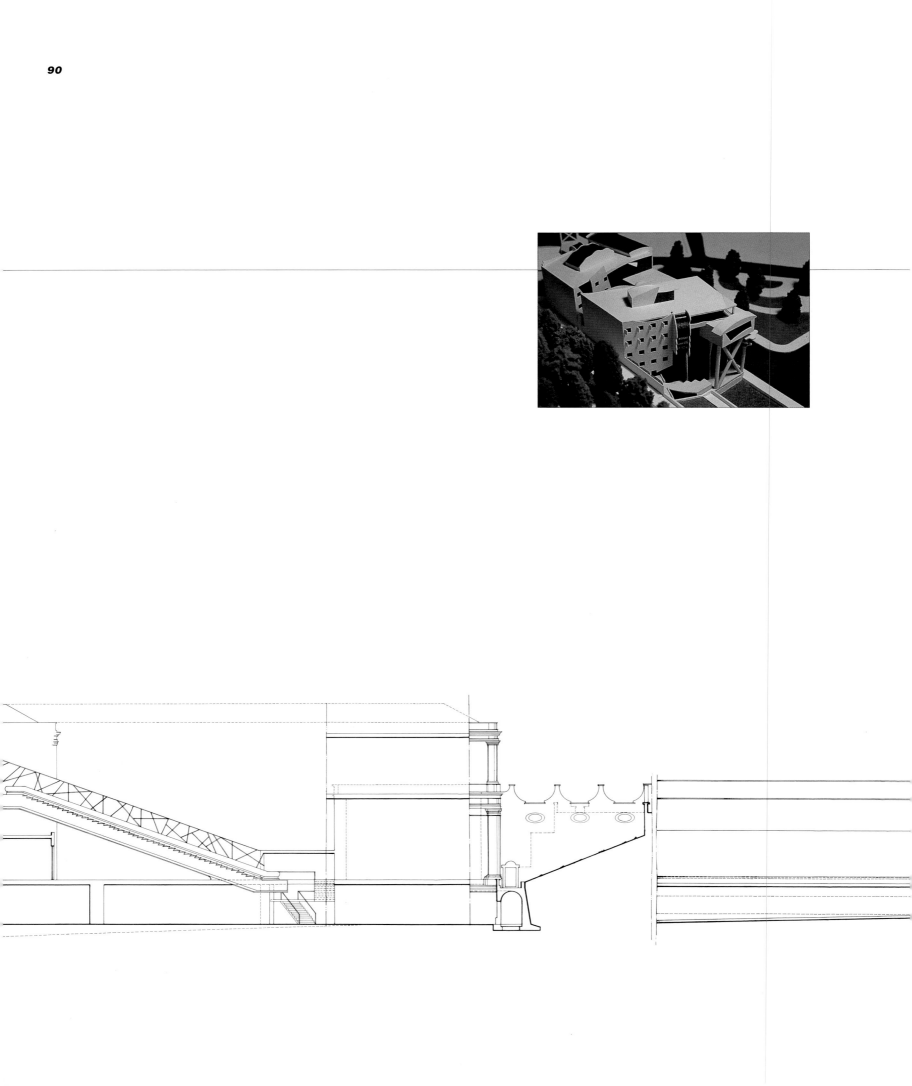

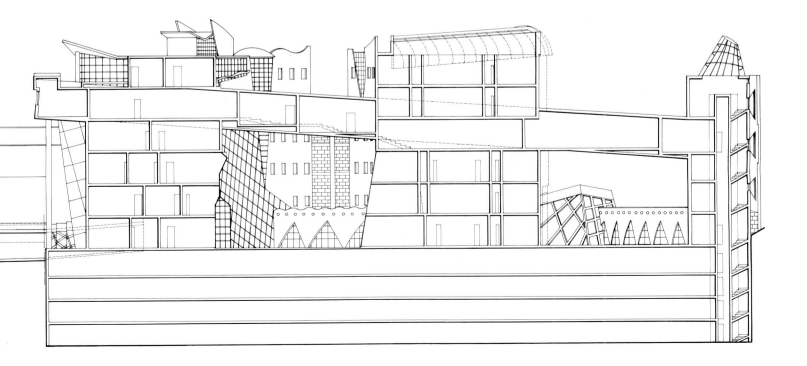

DORDRECHT PENITENTIARY (DICK TRACY BUILDING)

This was for a limited competition organised by the public works ministry of the Dutch Government who invited three architects, Tomás Taveira, Vittorio Gregotti and WJ Neutelings to participate.

The objective was to propose new ideas for a prison, whilst assuming all the rules of freedom limitation, movement limitation and visual control.

Dordrecht is a small town near Rotterdam with a rehabilitated old centre and notable characteristics such as the canals and the historical Dutch perfume.

The design pursued the idea of making a prison in the form of a small town, where one could find 'plazas', streets, local entertainment and various meeting points. Each building possessed its own colour, its individual form and was not ashamed of the nature of the project.

Although no one received first prize in this competition it was a rewarding experience to have participated.
(*Dordrecht, the Netherlands, 1993*)

Design sketches and front elevation; PAGES 94-95: Ground floor plan and side elevation; PAGES 96-97: Design sketches; PAGES 98-99: Second floor plan and rear elevation; PAGES 100-101: Third floor plan; PAGES 102-103: Axonometric and side elevation; PAGES 104-105: Cross- and longitudinal sections

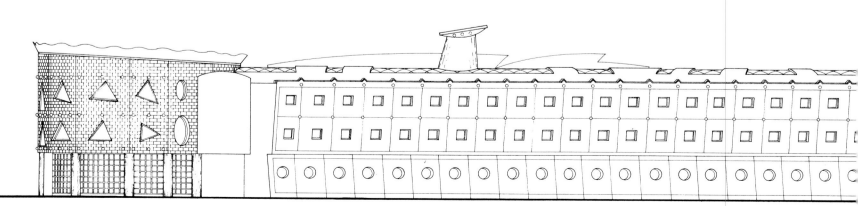

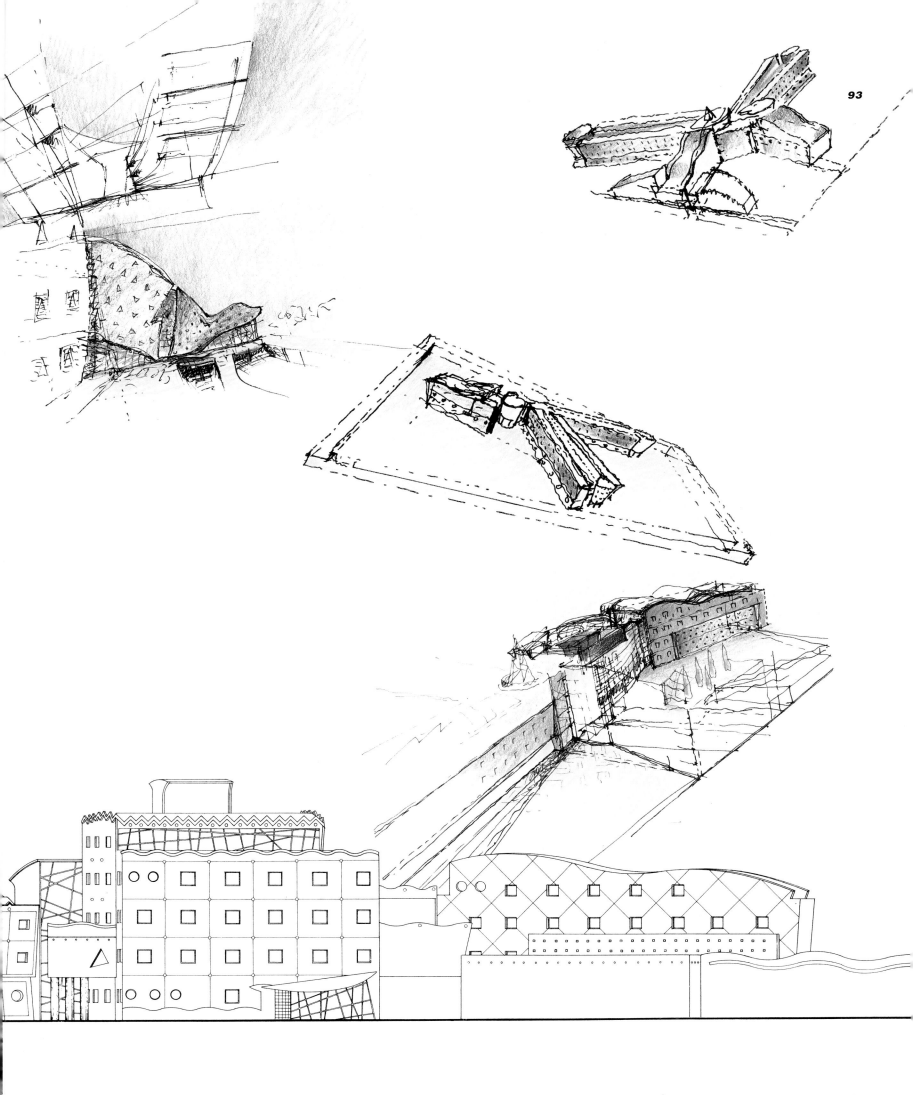

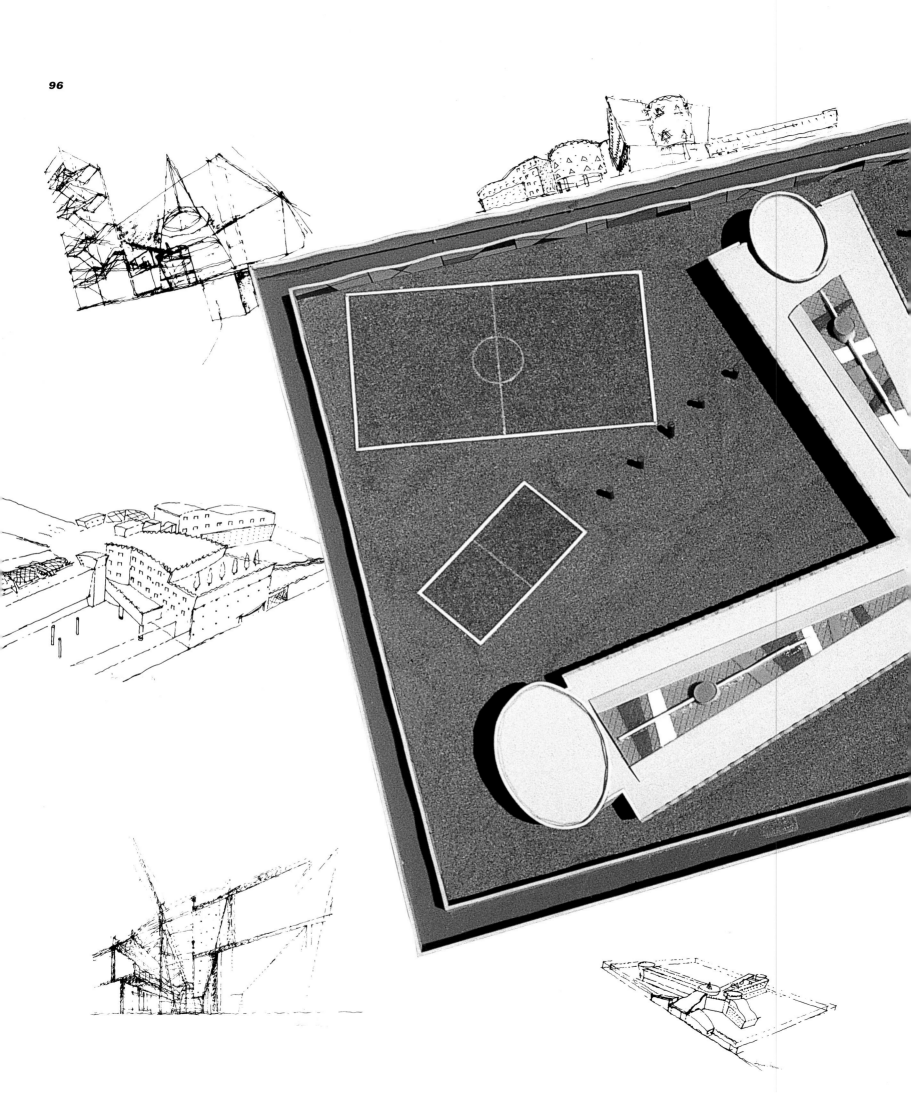

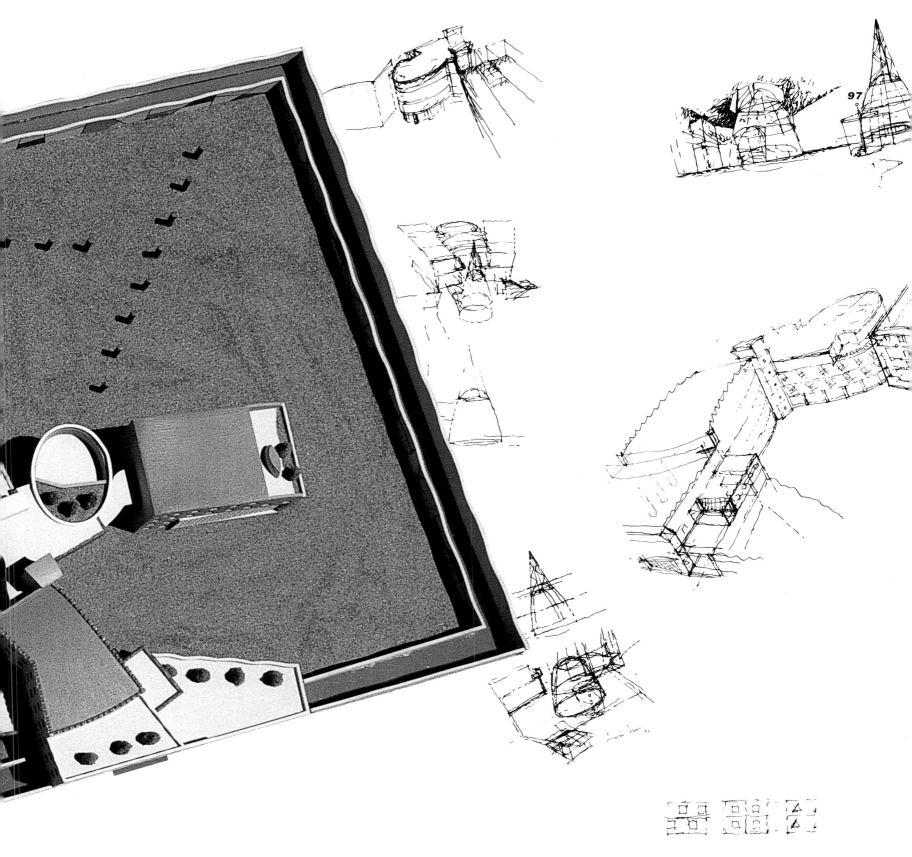

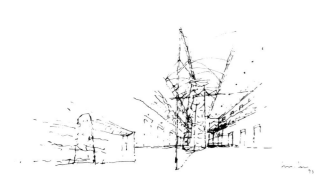

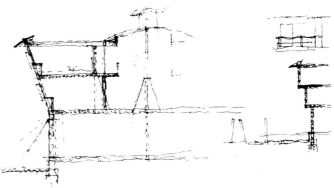

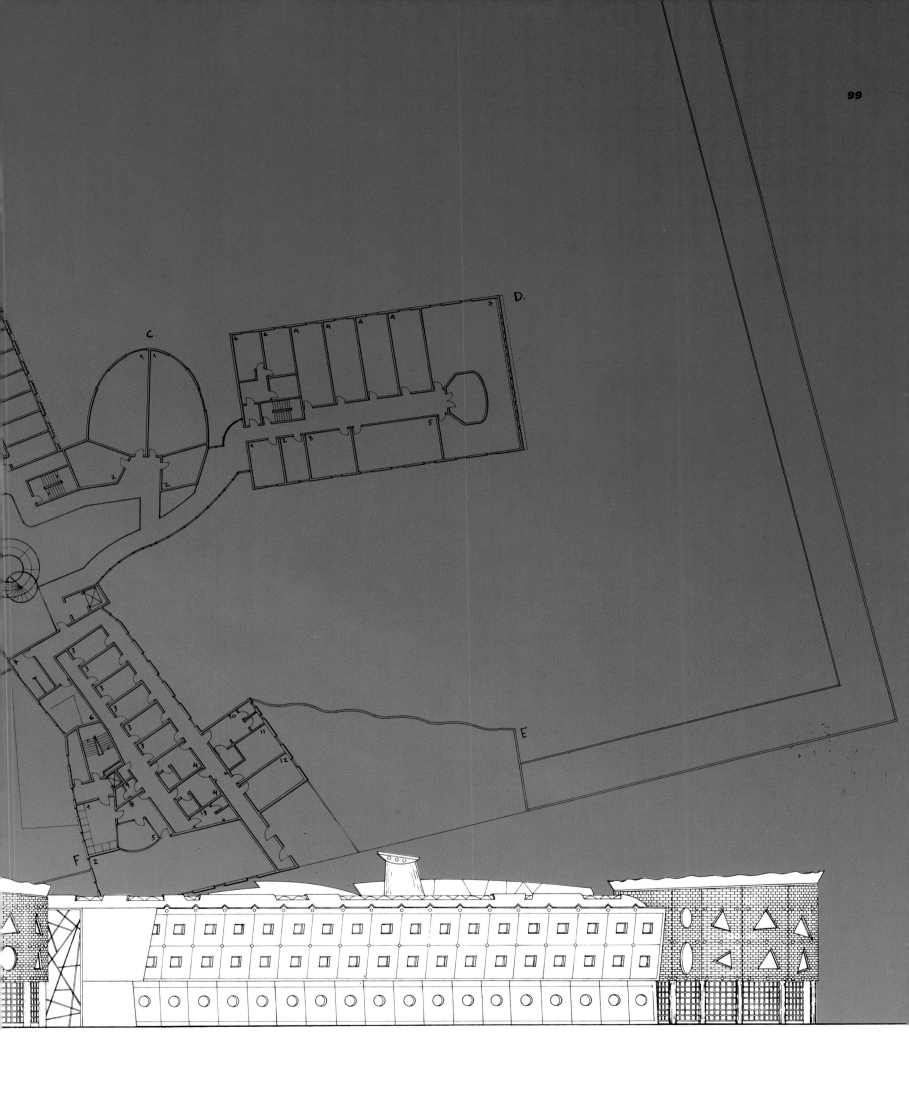

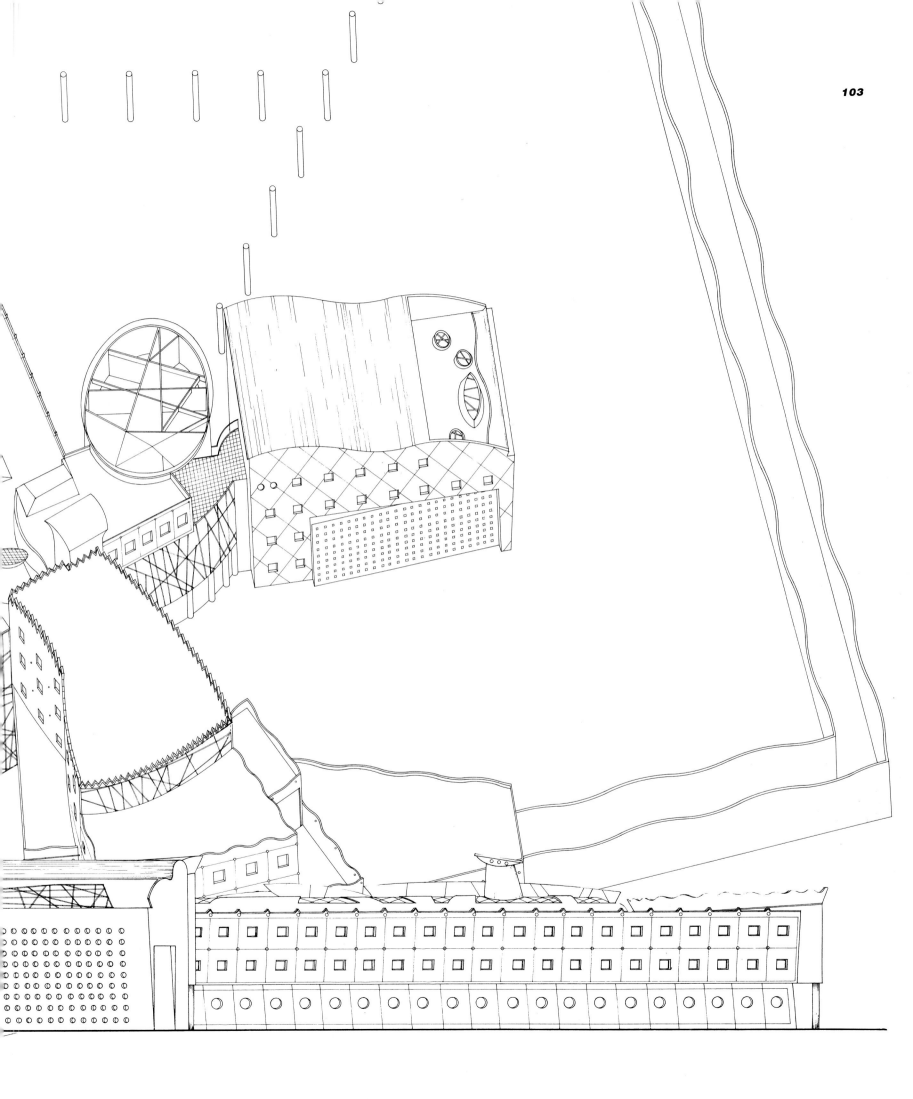

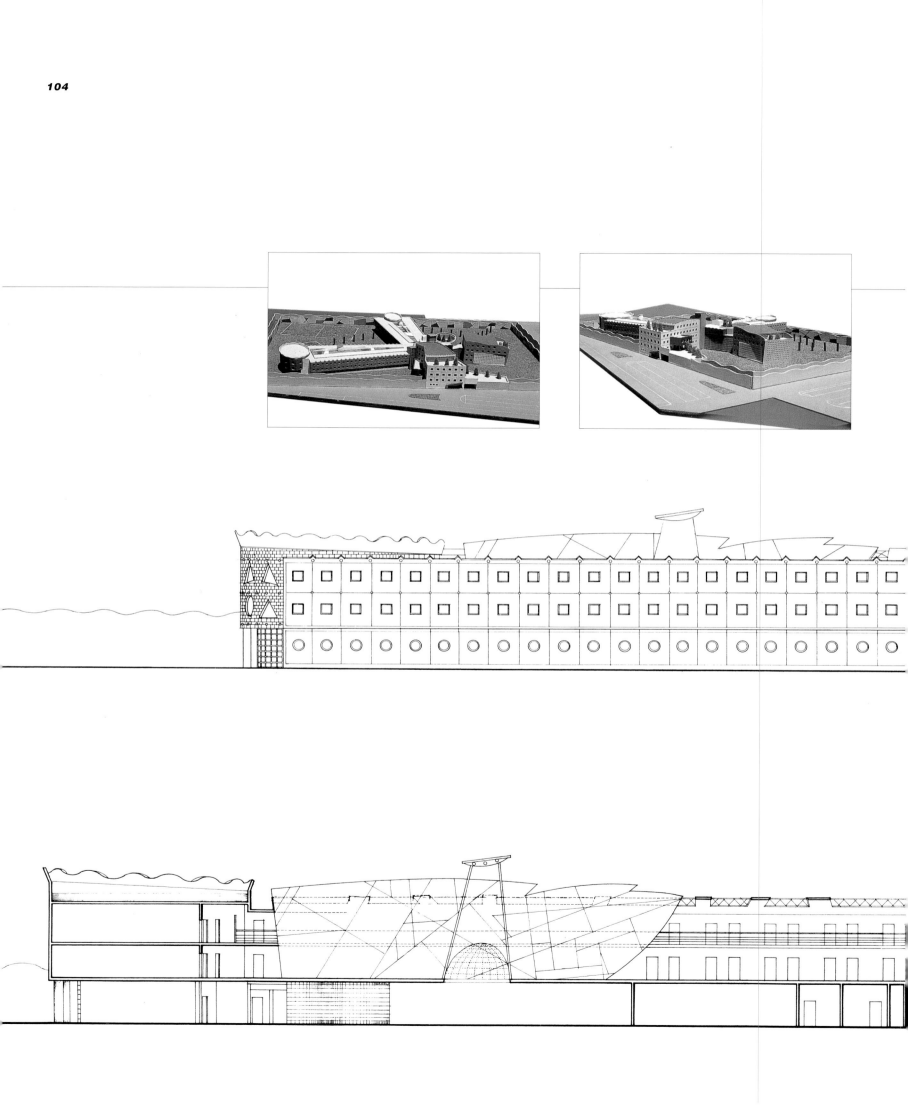

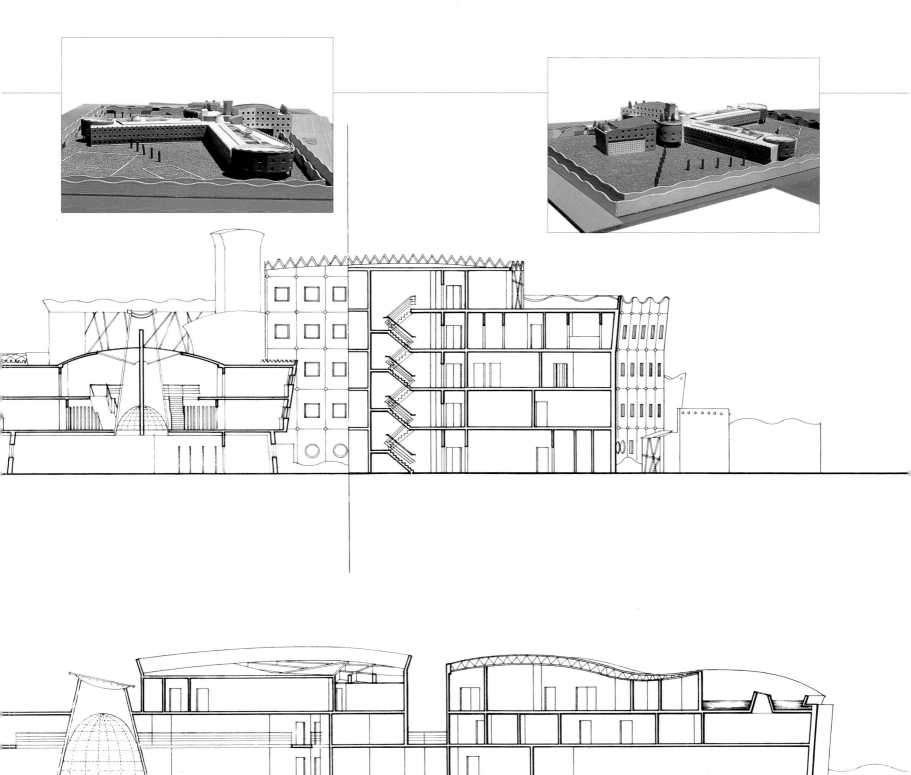

METRO CITY

This project fulfils the new strategy of the metro state owned company which, in the new Lisbon metro stations, wishes to create a commercial structure and a space where affiliated commercial firms can fulfil their financial objective.

In fact, in each metro station one can find space for advertising which takes advantage of the number of people using each station to sell goods.

Following the metro company strategy, the architect's idea was to create a shopping centre as well as an advertising centre surrounding a metro station, and to give it a beautiful atmosphere by using canopies, through which natural light illuminates every part.

In addition car parking is available for 500 cars, above and below ground; making the total area of the complex almost 65,000 m².
(*Lisbon, Portugal*)

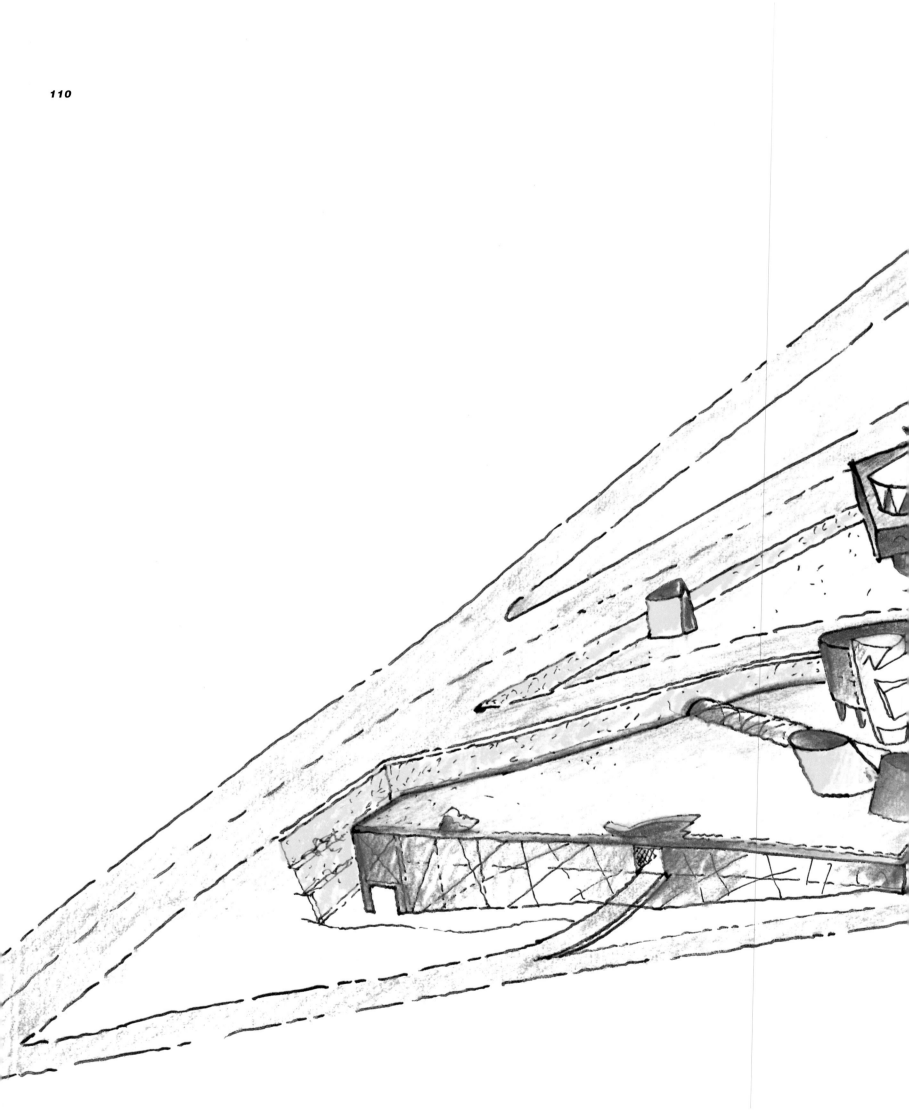

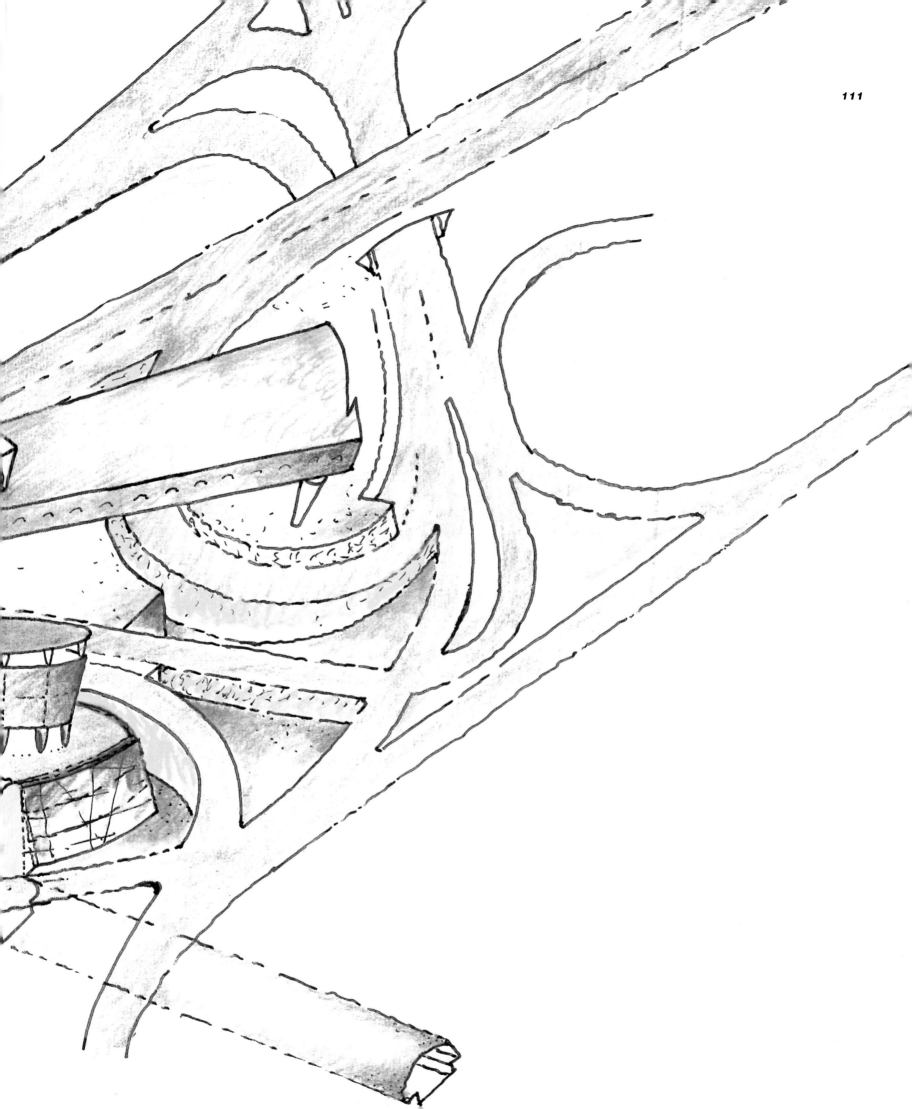

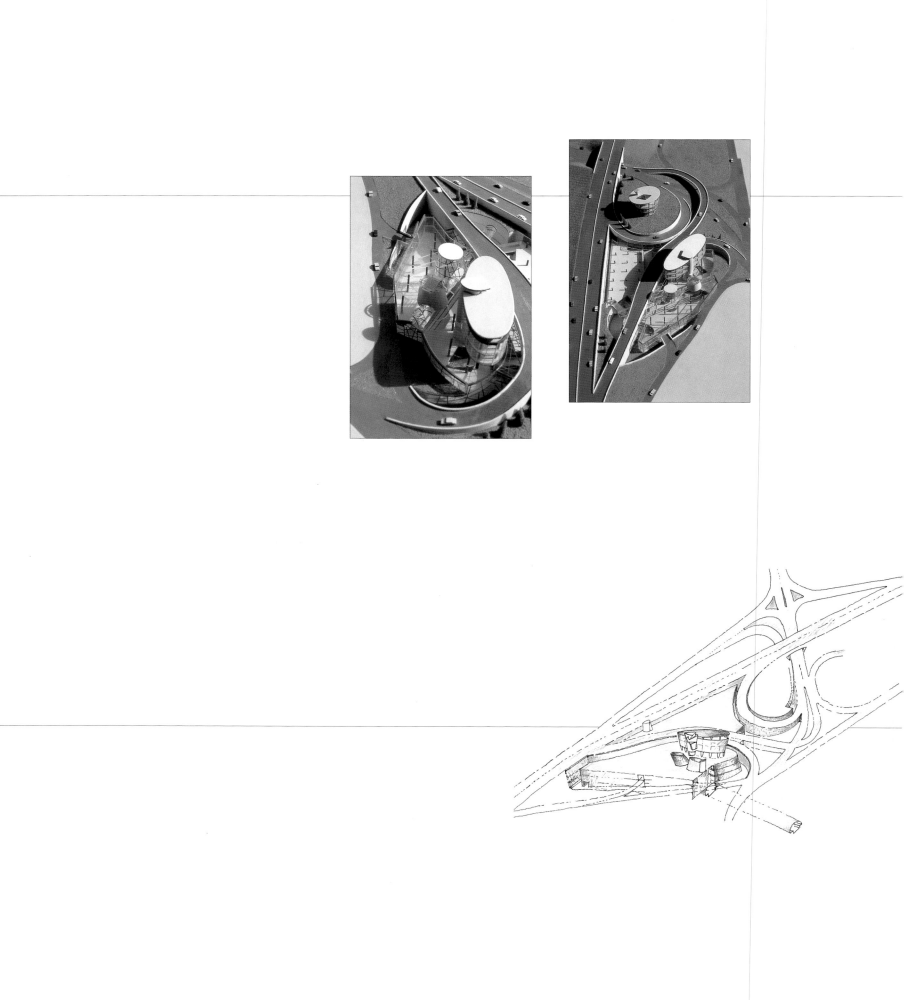

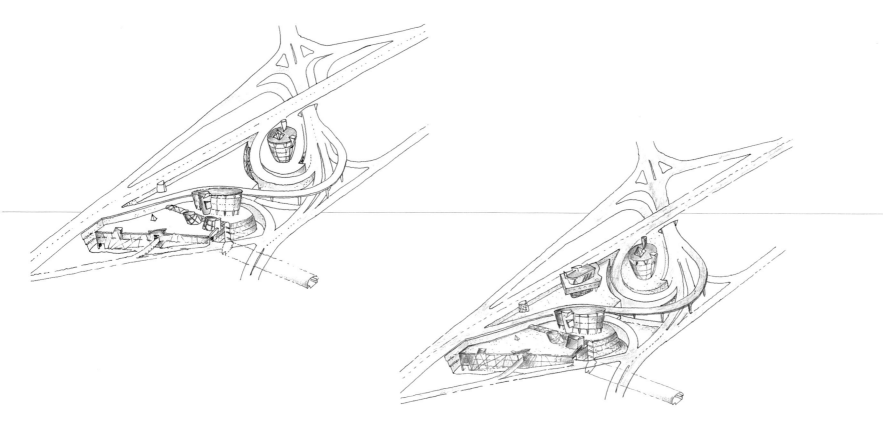

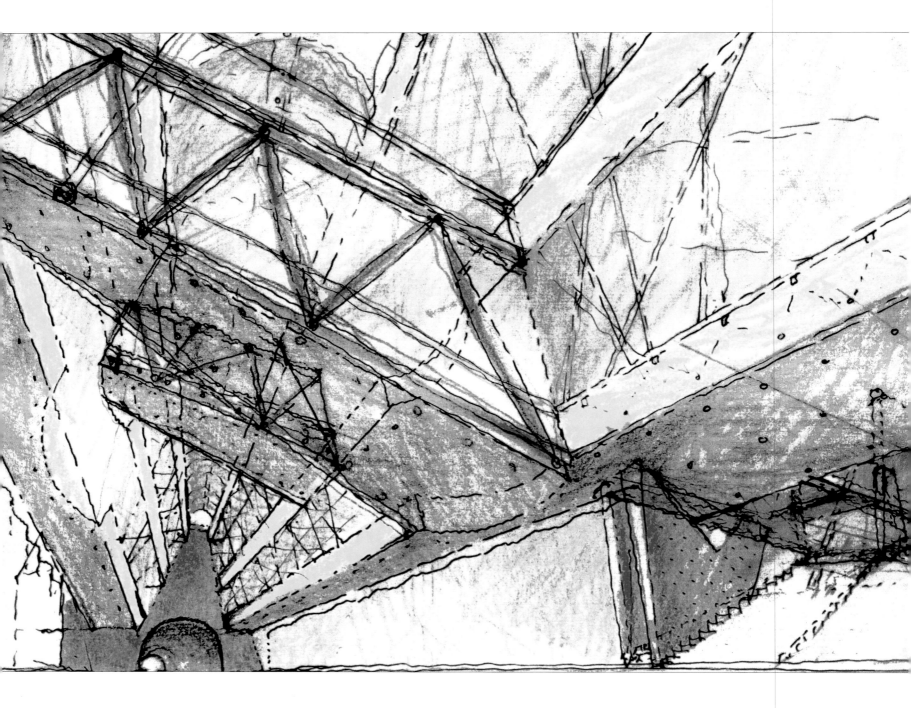

PP1 URBAN PLAN, EXPO 98

This is an urban plan of the central area of the EXPO 98 which is organised by the Portuguese Government. Located in Lisbon, EXPO 98 faces the Tagus River, which until recently was the site of the most important industrial buildings. This area, comprising 310 hectares, will be rebuilt to accommodate new housing, multipurpose buildings, shopping areas and leisure areas, including river sports. It is widely regarded as being one of the most important urban developments in Lisbon.

The lack of space to accommodate new development and a decreasing local population, led the Lisbon government and commerce to seize the opportunity which the EXPO 98 offered. It gave them the chance to reurbanise the surroundings as a new central urban cluster.

As winners of the competition to put forward a design plan for the development, the architects were commissioned to carry out the scheme. This is the preliminary study finished in August 94.

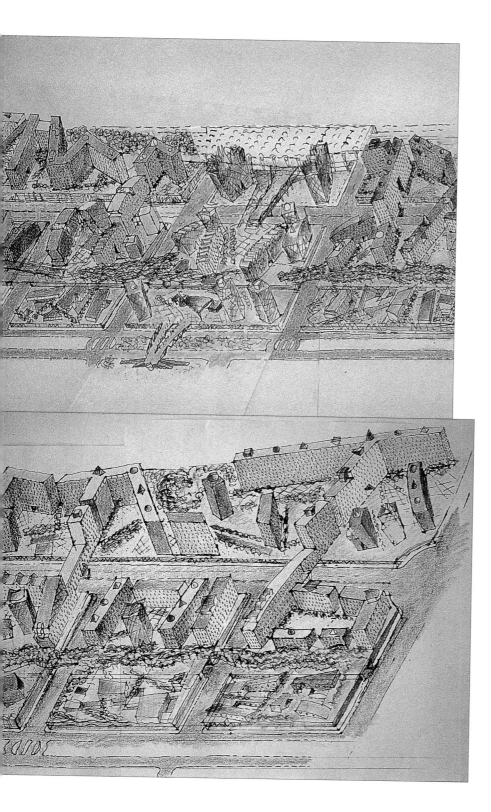

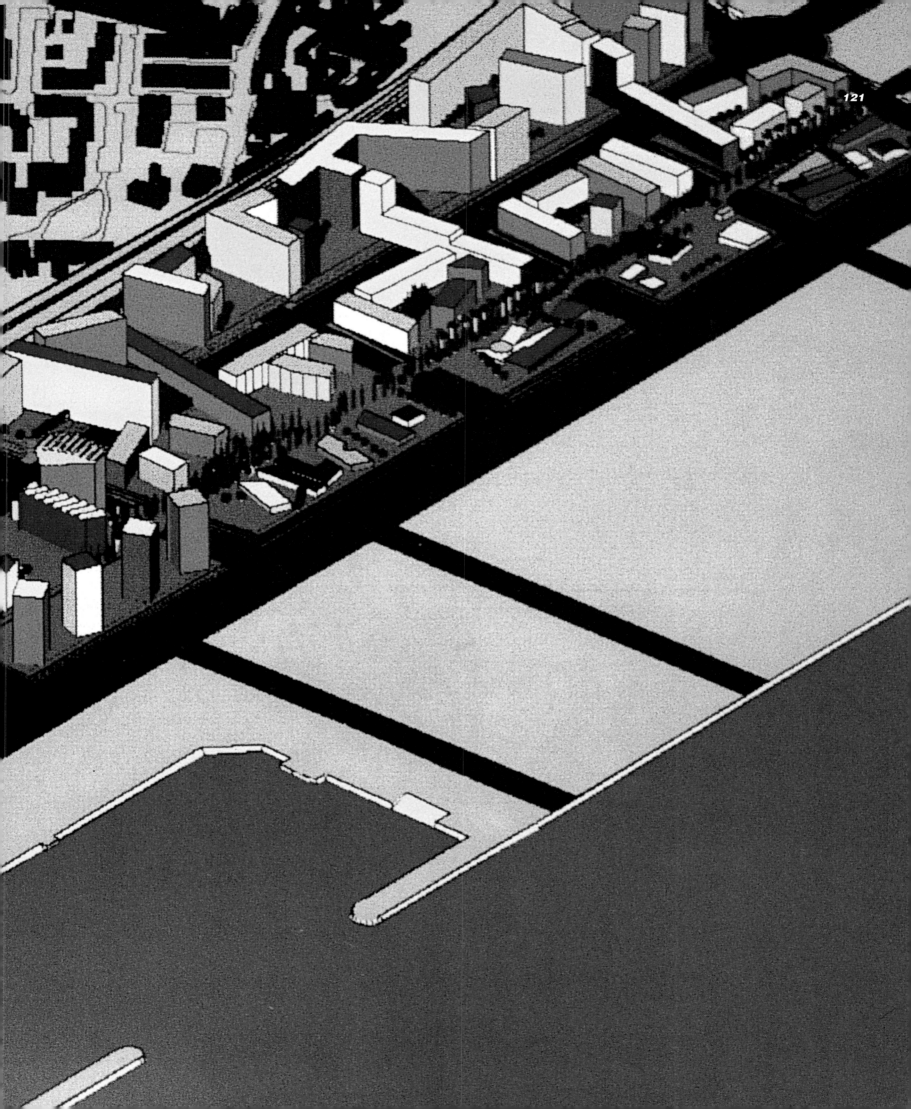

Taveira's executed designs can be seen to prolong his architectural investigation. Only recently was Taveira's considerable experience with transfigured objects utilised to support a more serious and intentional design.

The experience of designing a chair integrated with a group of architects and designers such as Hans Hollein, Jorge Pensi, Antonio Citerio and Jasper Morrison was highly rewarding, due to the fact that the architect was obliged to produce a design under great contention.

For Taveira, design will always be an exercise of excitement as well as an opportunity to produce new objects laden with art which is also functional.
(Lisbon, Portugal, 1987-94)

PAGES 122-25: Stage design for Figueira da Foz music festival, 1987; PAGES 126-27: TV programme, In Bed with Alexandra Lencastre, *1994; PAGES 128-31: Transfigurations, crockery designs, 1989; PAGES 132-33: 'Rick' chair, 1989; PAGES 134-35: 'Sandeman' chair, 1989; PAGE 136: 'Marcello' chair, 1985; PAGE 137: 'Silvia' chair, 1990; PAGES 136-37: 'Maria' chair; PAGE 138: 'Don Pedro' chair, 1993; 'Dona Inês' chair, 1993; 'Don João' chairs, 1993; PAGE 139: 'Olaias' chair, 1993; 'Lucia' chair, 1993; 'Marilyn I' sofa, 1994; 'Marilyn III' sofa, 1994; PAGES 140-41: Different versions of 'Laura' chair, 1993; 'Laura' chair sketches; PAGES 142-43: 'Fernando Pessoa' sofas, 1993*

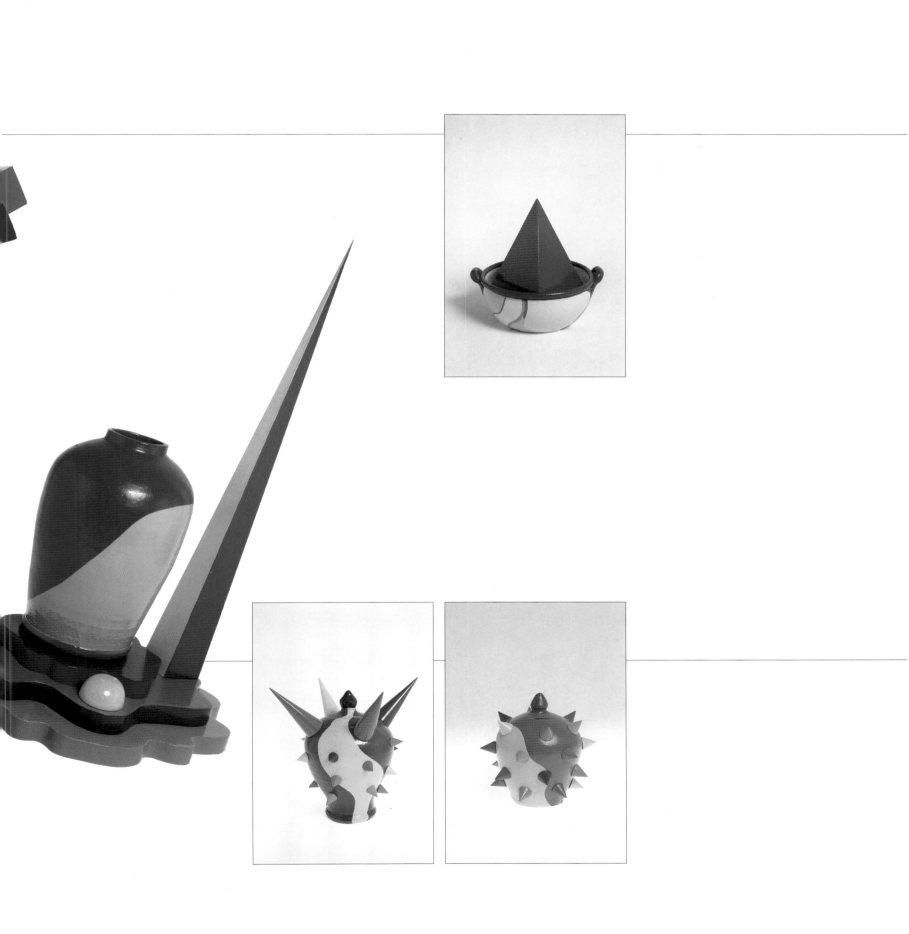

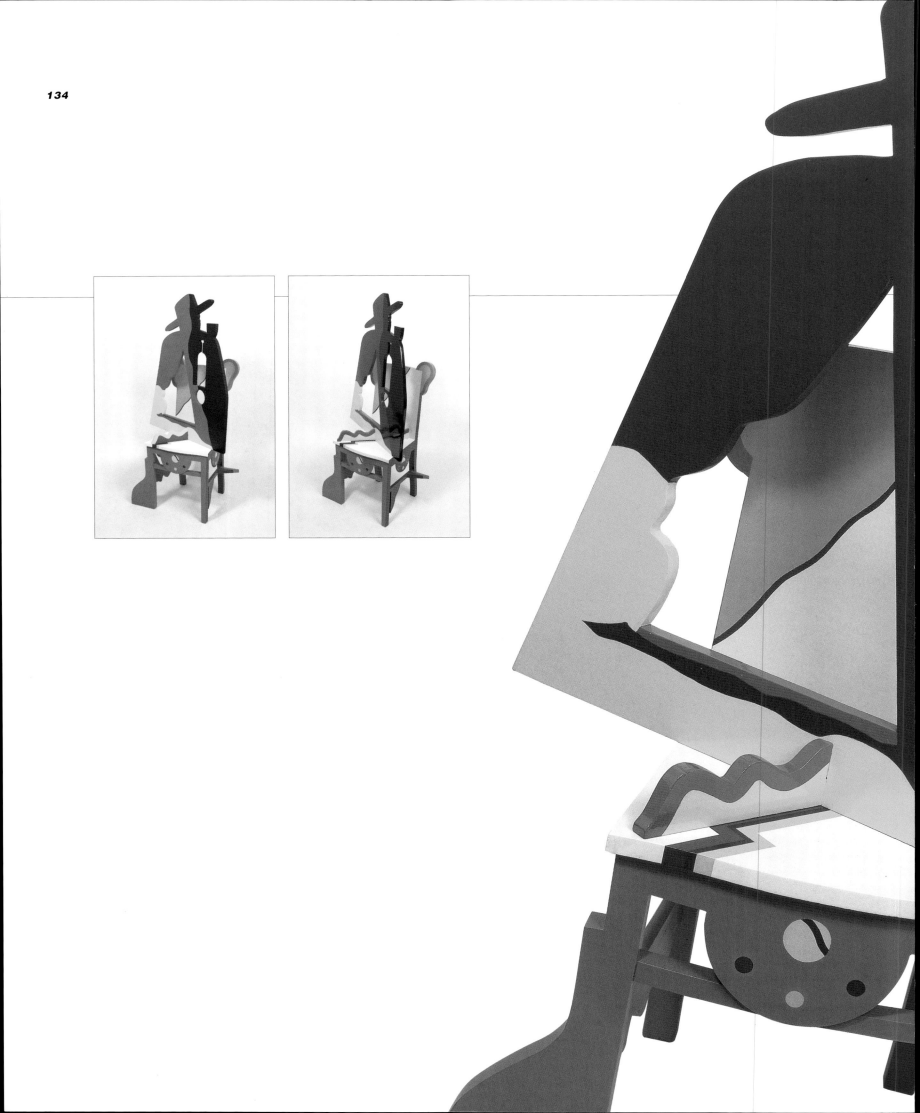

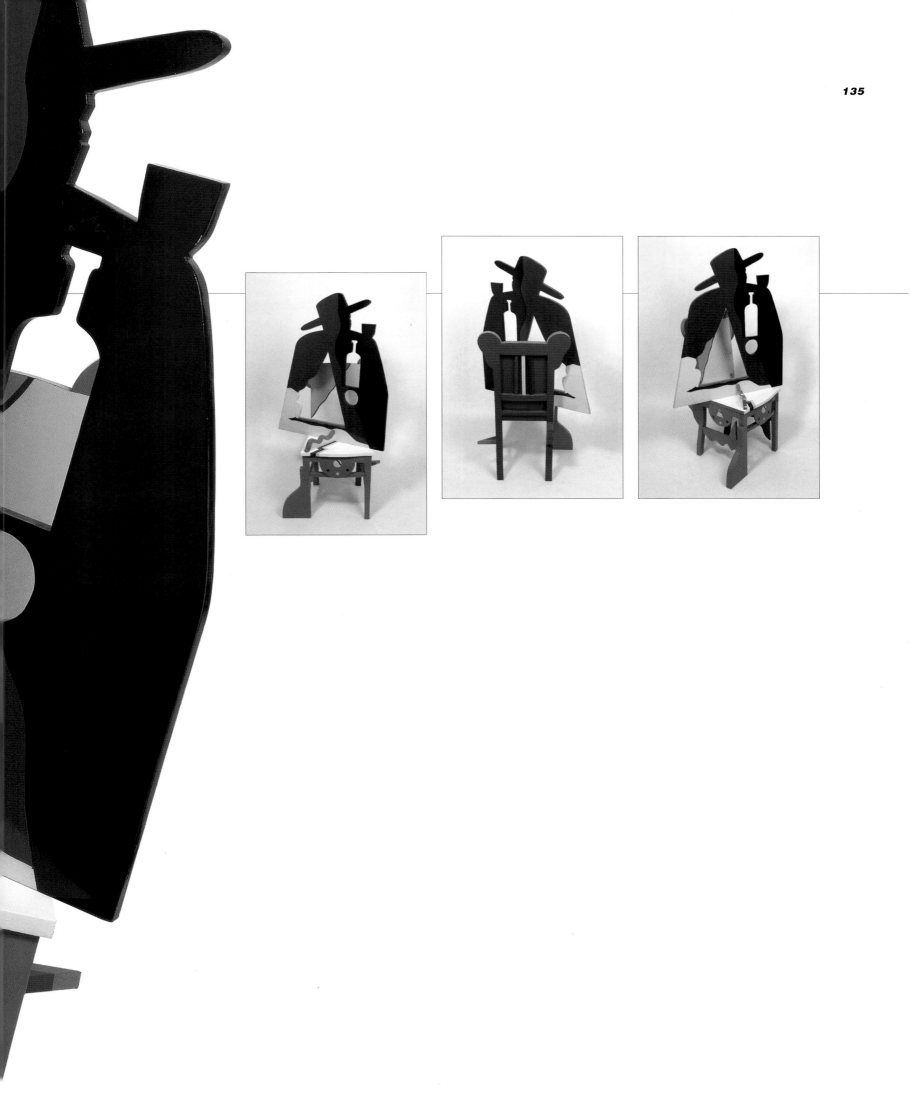

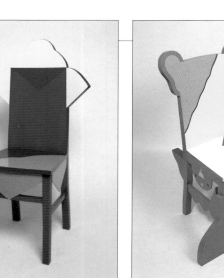

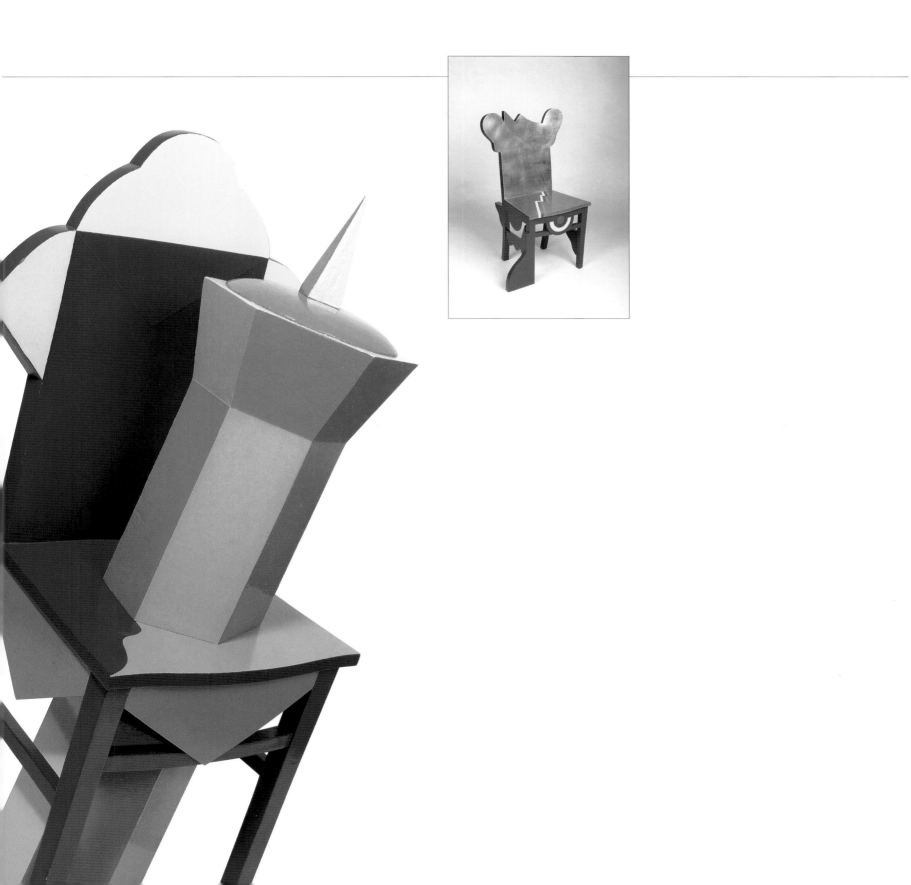

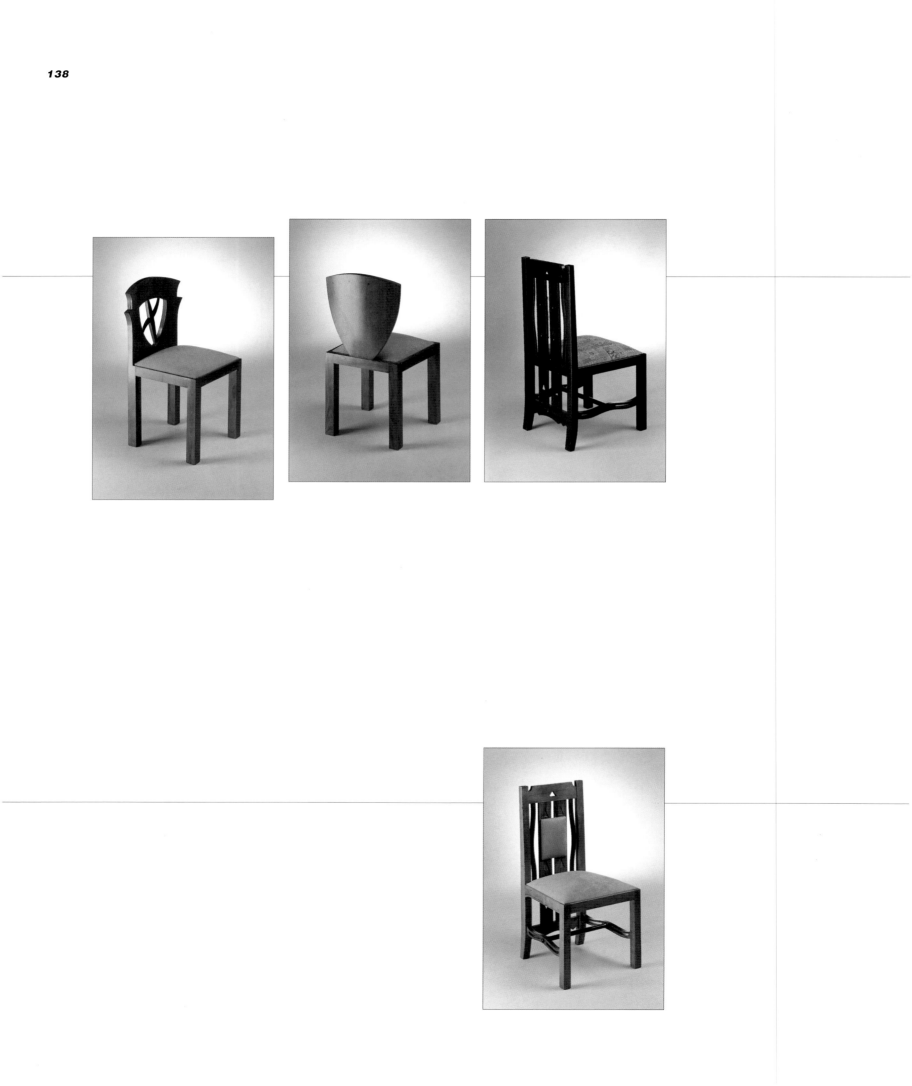

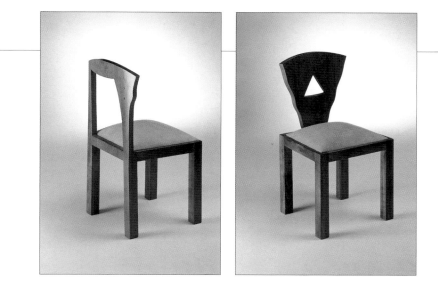

BIOGRAPHY

Tomás Cardoso Taveira, ESBAL (Lisbon School of Fine Arts) Architect and Planner. 1977-78: MIT (Spurs Programme) 1971 to present:

• Professor at Lisbon School of Architecture

• Organiser of the Lisbon International Architectural Symposium annually

• Exhibitions of drawings in Madrid (Arco 85 and 86).

• Exhibition of *Transfigured Objects*, Lisbon 85 (Galeria Cómicos)

• Exhibition of *Transfigured Objects and Architectural Projects and Drawings*, Oporto 1986 and Lisbon (Amoreiras Shopping Centre) 1986

• Architectural exhibitions in Buenos Aires, Madrid, Barcelona, Rio de Janeiro, Málaga, Strasbourg

• Conferences in different Universities around the world

• Participation in Chicago Neocon 18 (1986) with Ricardo Bofill, Cesar Pelli, Charles Moore and Mario Botta

• Author of two books *Discourse of the City* (1974) and *Martim Moniz Urban Renewal* (1982); National Academy of Fine Arts Award, (1982) Lisbon Council Architectural Award (1982); Valmor Award (1982).

Taveira writes for newspapers and magazines. His work has been included in publications such as *Progressive Architecture*, *Domus*, *Ambiente*, *A+U*, *International Herald Tribune*, *New York Times*, *Libération*. He has architectural works in Portugal, Saudi Arabia, United Arab Emirates, Macau, Angola and Cabo Verde.

Taveira is a member of the American Institute of Planners; International Union of Architects and International Association of Art Critics.

Academy Editions (London) also published a book on his work in 1991.